FAMILY & KINSHIP IN MODERN SOCIETY

Bernard Farber
Arizona State University

SCOTT, FORESMAN
INTRODUCTION TO MODERN SOCIETY SERIES

Albert J. Reiss, Jr.
Harold L. Wilensky

Editors

Scott, Foresman and Company

GLENVIEW, ILLINOIS   BRIGHTON, ENGLAND

Cover Acknowledgment: © Museum of Modern Art, A Conger Goodyear Fund.

Library of Congress Catalog Card Number: 72-84788
ISBN: 0-673-05963-4

Regional Offices of Scott, Foresman and Company are located in
Dallas, Texas; Glenview, Illinois; Oakland, New Jersey; Palo Alto,
California; Tucker, Georgia; and Brighton, England.

FAMILY & KINSHIP IN MODERN SOCIETY

Foreword

Modern societies are complex territorial organizations whose populations are more-or-less integrated by economic, legal, military, and political institutions and by the meda of mass communication and entertainment. Sociology reflects this complexity. It is often packaged in separate sociologies such as those of work, religion, minorities, politics, and the community.

By looking at modernization as a process, and urban-industrial ("modern" "affluent") society as a distinctive social system, this series hopes to avoid fragmentation into separate sociologies and at the same time provide intensive treatment of major institutional areas (economy, polity, kinship), units of social organization (society, community, complex organization, family), and of processes that cut across all institutional areas (social differentiation and stratification, social control, demographic and technological change). The series is "relevant" in that all authors address themselves to a single question: "What is modern about modern society?" It is comparative in that all authors know that we cannot answer that question unless we compare the different shapes of modern and premodern societies and of contemporary nations, totalitarian and pluralist, "capitalist" and "socialist." Our abiding concern is the macroscopic, comparative analysis of social structure and change.

Each book in this series can stand alone for specialized courses; each can also be used in combination with others as a flexible substitute for conventional textbooks.

In this introduction to modern kinship systems, Bernard Farber views the family as a property system. From his perspective, we see relatives as one's valued property as well as means for increasing or maintaining one's own worth in the society. Assuming that there are typical ways of delimiting and using relatives in every society, Farber traces changes in America and Western Europe in norms governing the definition and rights of relatives. He finds a shift from the "natural-family" to a "legal-family" model.

Although many scholars see this shift as a sign of greater democratization and equalitarianism in modern life, Farber argues instead that it portends a threat to traditional civil liberties.

As long as the nuclear family was considered a "natural" or sacred domain, whose charter for existence was regarded as independent of the state, there were many legal protections against encroachment upon the household. The home was a private domain, safe from search and seizure by the state. However, the legal-family paradigm treats the family as a sub-unit of the state and therefore subject to various legal restrictions and to intrusion by government agents (e.g., social workers and law enforcement officers).

The book follows modifications in family law through American and, to a lesser extent, through European history. It focuses primarily on laws pertaining to marriage and divorce, support of indigent relatives, illegitimacy, adoption, and intestacy. There is a parallel discussion of changes in American society over the past two centuries. The book suggests that increasing diversification in family norms is required to accommodate the effects of tumultuous historical events (such as war and economic depression), economic and technological development, and demographic processes; these social factors have created the conditions for the emergence of the legal-family paradigm.

The waning of the family as a protected domain has, in addition, implications for the persistence of specific norms and values. The loss of the conception of familial protectedness leads to serious questioning in the society of traditional, prevalent family and kinship systems. In consequence, there is much instability of family life-styles, including a weakening of the marriage bond. Farber foresees continuing diversification and revision of familial norms in modern society, which is organized in ways consistent with the legal-family paradigm.

Farber offers a creative contribution to the study of modern kinship. His book is unique in (1) its viewpoint of family and kinship as a property system (instead of regarding the family as a small group organized around a set of functions), (2) its use of family law as data in the analysis of historical trends, and (3) its emphasis on kinship analysis as an integral aspect of family study.

Albert J. Reiss, Jr.
Harold L. Wilensky

Preface

Perhaps the best way to describe this book is to say what it is *not.*
First, although it relies heavily on family law as a source of data, it
is not a legal textbook. The book does not pretend to provide an
exhaustive and systematic treatment of statutes and court decisions on all aspects of law related to the family. Such topics as
abortion, community property, child abuse, and husband-wife
obligations are omitted, and those topics that are included are
analyzed from a social science perspective.

Second, while the book regards family law and the American
family from a historical viewpoint, it is not a history of the family.
If it were, it would have to deal with variations in family forms for
different social strata and different epochs. Rather, the history in
this book is aimed at showing broad changes in dominant family
norms to indicate the revolutionary character of recent social
phenomena in the United States and Western Europe.

The book does discuss the fundamental role of family and
kinship in the destiny of Western society. In doing so, it makes
use of family law to indicate trends in basic paradigms of family
and kinship prevalent in our society. In this context, the term
paradigm refers to conceptual models of the ways in which family
and kinship groups are organized and the manner in which they
are supposed to operate. Naturally, the assumption is made that
there is some correspondence between the legal statement in
statutes or in court decisions and the prevailing paradigms.

The references listed in the footnotes and Selected Readings
do not include the statutes for the fifty states. Although there are
numerous references in the text to specific sections and para-
graphs in state codes, I decided that it would be superfluous to
describe them in detail. For each state, I have used the most recent
compilation of revised statutes, along with 1970 supplements.
The historical analyses of laws in the text refer to the statutes
listed in the Appendix.

I want to acknowledge the research assistance in this project
of Michael Benson, Mrs. Roberta Slivken Cohen, Marshall Farkas,
and Elizabeth Koschka, as well as the secretarial skills of Mrs.
Sharon Cook of the University of Illinois and the typing staff at
Arizona State University. I am grateful to all of them.

Tempe, Arizona   B. F.

CONTENTS

Kinship as a Resource

What is meant by the term *family?* What is the role of the family in society? Both questions are related: how one answers the first question will in part determine his response to the second. Each of us has some idea of what "family" is, and we also have some notion of what we think about family obligations, family duties, the conditions under which divorce is permissible, ways of raising children, and so on. But despite an intuitive grasp of the concept of "family," we may not realize how our disparate thoughts can be organized into a coherent model of family structure or how our own conceptual "mapping" of the family compares with general cultural *paradigms[1] in the society. Using legal codes and landmark court decisions as a basis, this book will describe cultural models of family and kinship organization in the United States and thereby try to assess the significance of changes in family law for understanding the development of modern social structure.

[1] Throughout this book, an asterisk before a word when it first appears indicates that the term is defined in the Glossary, pp. 159–164.

DEFINITION OF FAMILY

To perform this task, it will first be necessary to present two alternative definitions of the family: (a) the family defined as a small group consisting of parents and their non-adult children living in a single household—the *nuclear family—and (b) the family defined as a cluster of people, whose relationship is stipulated by law in terms of marriage and *descent, and whose precise membership varies according to the circumstances. The first definition is based on *function* as a mechanism for generating modes of organization of family members; the second utilizes the concept of *property rights* in family members as a propelling force in organization. The first definition is the one traditionally applied by social scientists to the study of the family and, as the analysis in this book will suggest, it is the one which is appropriate for describing the cultural paradigm implied in nineteenth-century family law; for reasons that should become apparent in later chapters, the second definition more realistically depicts the paradigm of family organization expressed in modern law. After a brief discussion of the first definition, we will in this chapter treat the second definition more fully.

Family and Universal Functions

The functionalist approach to the study of the family originated in the effort of social anthropologists to find universal attributes in family life. Radcliffe-Brown[2] and his followers have regarded the family as a nuclear (or conjugal) unit in which *norms of interaction are governed by a set of functions which it performs in all societies. Usually, such universal functions have included the procreation of children, socialization of children, management of sex relations of the parents (and incestuous prohibitions for children), and organization of household economy.[3] This view emphasizes the universality of the family as a unique system of social relationships resulting from the interplay of these functions.

Other functionalists place less importance upon the systemic aspects of these functions and stress the individual functions

[2]   A. R. Radcliffe-Brown and Daryll Forde, eds., *African Systems of Kinship and Marriage* (New York: Oxford University Press, 1950), esp. pp. 1–85.

[3]   George P. Murdock, *Social Structure* (New York: Macmillan, 1949).

themselves in shaping *values, norms, and *roles in family and kinship. For example, Malinowski regards the crucial function of the family to be that of defining the *social status of the individual, that is, his place in the economic, political, and religious life of the community. For Malinowski, the sociological significance of the father stems from this status-providing function.[4]

Among those social scientists who regard the family as deriving from universal functions, there is a general agreement that changes in technology and the economy stimulate new routines and eliminate others within the family. These newly created routines may require family members to adapt to changes in circumstance by migrating, reorganizing their daily regimen, or developing new interpersonal life styles associated with professional or business advancement. The theory is that through these adaptations, the roles of parents and children are reorganized to fulfill family functions effectively in a new setting. This adaptive process establishes a "fit" between the requirements of an industrial system and the form of the family.

Those social scientists who focus more on individual functions than on the interplay of functions are somewhat less optimistic about the viability of family life in modern society. As economic, religious, educational, and other activities of family life are being transferred to other institutions, these scientists say, the family becomes an increasingly specialized institution. In fact, in the first part of the twentieth century, some sociologists (like Sorokin)[5] saw the family dwindling away, losing its functions to other institutions, until at last there would be no family.

The analysis of laws in this book will suggest that there is a close resemblance between the sociological conception that the family is based on universal functions and the cultural model that the nuclear family is a "natural" entity, viable under all social conditions. These two complementary views dominated sociological and legal thought until the middle of the twentieth century. They influenced even those sociologists who described the nuclear family as withering away and perhaps prevented them from discerning the emergence of new cultural models.

[4] Bronislaw Malinowski, "Parenthood—the Basis of Social Structure," in *Sourcebook in Marriage and the Family*, Marvin B. Sussman, ed. (Boston: Houghton Mifflin, 1963, 2nd ed.), pp. 40–48.

[5] Pitirim A. Sorokin, *Social and Cultural Dynamics* (New York: Harper and Brothers, 1937), Vol. 4, p. 776.

Family and Property Rights

The alternative sociological conception of the family as a set of property rights reverses the basic problem set forth by the universal-functions approach. The functional approach starts with the supposition that certain activities, necessary for the society to continue to exist, are performed most efficiently by the nuclear family; hence, the nuclear family is ubiquitous as a recognizable, functioning entity. The alternative position starts with the assumption that people exist as networks of relatives who have claims on one another; it then asks how people use these relatives. The functionalists thus begin with necessary actions, while the alternative is to begin with people who have biological ties.

The biological acts of sexual intercourse and birth have everywhere generated norms and values that deal with the relatedness of people. Sometimes these acts have resulted in ephemeral relationships, such as makeshift child-care arrangements or short love affairs, but beyond these brief interludes, every society has evolved stable family and kinship structures which enable it to continue. As later discussion will indicate, the stabilization of sexual relationships provides the basis for defining reciprocities associated with the institution of marriage. These reciprocities involve not only the married couple but also persons related to them. In addition, the act of birth creates the necessity of establishing rules for determining responsibility for children over their life cycle, i.e., as they mature into adulthood, marry, procreate, age, and die; these responsibilities reflect the individual's concern for those related to him by descent. The claims established through marriage and descent thereby create for each individual a reservoir of relatives from whom he can anticipate certain kinds of conduct associated with "family" or "kinship" in the society in which he lives. The extent and nature of these claims vary from one society to another.

Societies make use of biological kinship in different ways. In some societies, categories of kinship may be applied in ways which sustain a highly *differentiated system of social stratification; in others, the organization of kinship relations may be oriented toward *integrating family units on a basis of equality. This difference in utilization of kinship as a resource will influence norms pertaining to marriages between people from different segments of society, the kinds of socialization practices adopted, matters of guardianship and household management, patterns of inheritance, and the relationship between familial and other institutions in the society.

PARTITIONING OF KIN AS PROPERTY

One problem faced by every society is how to partition groups of family and kin in order to use their connectedness in structuring social relationships. Societies have developed several biological criteria for partitioning kin, but not every society, of course, uses all these characteristics or processes as criteria for partitioning. These criteria include:[6]
1. *Affinity and *consanguinity (i.e., whether the relationship exists through marriage or birth)
2. Generation or birth cohort (i.e., whether a relative is in an *ascending, *descending, or *collateral generation)
3. Sex differences between male and female
4. Collaterality (i.e., closeness of the relationship, often in degrees of closeness)
5. Bifurcation (i.e., whether linkage to a particular person is through male or female connecting relatives)
6. Decedence (i.e., whether the death of a person extinguishes the kinship ties between persons for whom he had provided a connecting link)
There are numerous activities for which partitioning of relatives may be significant (e.g., performance of ritual, economic cooperation). All societies require differentiation of kin with regard to (a) prohibitions on *incestuous marriage, (b) allocation of rights and duties of support, care, and responsibility for well-being of close relatives, and (c) succession (which involves inheritance) of property. Additional criteria exist for partitioning relatives, but these are generally derived from the biologically based criteria.[7]

Rules pertaining to incestuous marriage are particularly important for partitioning relatives in that they define classes of consanguineous and sometimes of affinal kinsman. These rules make use of the fact that the taboo on sexual intercourse between close relatives exists everywhere. The basis for this prohibition

[6] Murdock, *Social Structure.*

[7] One criterion is polarity, i.e., whether two relatives are linguistically identical or reciprocal. For example, "cousins" form an identical class, but fathers versus sons form a reciprocal class.

has not been established empirically. Yet all major contributors to theories of family organization consider the incest taboo as a crucial element both in classifying relatives and in structuring society. There are differences in opinion as to why the incest taboo should be given serious attention in the study of the family. Some observers, like Murdock and Freud, regard the incest taboo primarily as a means of handling relationships within the nuclear family. In effect, their view is that the family has only an indirect influence on social structure; that is, the incest taboo requires only that nuclear family members marry outward, learn sexual inhibition, and resist those urges that would destroy the fundamental age-and-generation differentiation in the family. Aside from those resistive effects, the incest taboo (according to the nuclear-family explanation) permits the family to adapt to virtually all changes in social structure produced by economic, political, and religious institutions in the society. This explanation is essentially a psychological one, namely, that the incest taboo permits peace of mind (through avoidance of conflict and jealousy) together with the learning of instrumental orientations as distinguished from erotic orientations.

A second explanation is that the incest taboo is a mechanism which requires families to exchange members in marriage. Seen in this light, it functions as a direct influence on the nature of social structure. The reason for this influence, Lévi-Strauss suggests, is that the giving and taking of wives and husbands requires for such an exchange the organizing of kinship groups.[8] The form of exchange, then, molds the structure of the family and of kinship groups in the society. This conception of the incest taboo views family members primarily as property of the kin group (which emerges as a "corporation" to handle this property). Designations of who can be exchanged and how they are to be exchanged are defined by the rules of marriage. The form of marital exchange is then the archetype of the overall conception of exchange and reciprocity in the society. According to this explanation of the incest taboo, then, the fundamental problem in the development of social structure is that of exchange (or economic) relationships and not, as in the previous explanation, a matter of handling personal, psychological motivations.

A third conception of the incest taboo is that its purpose is to maintain the continuity of family and kinship groups as

---

[8] Claude Lévi-Strauss, *The Elementary Structures of Kinship* (Boston: Beacon Press, 1969).

proprietors of wealth, symbolic property, and members. The variations in persons covered by the incest taboo and the kinds of sanctions for violations define the strategies of family organization by which the society perpetuates *personal, *real, and *symbolic property. The incest taboo would then serve to protect the norms established to maintain this continuity. A *patrilineal society may place more stringent prohibitions upon sexual intercourse with the *wives* of kinsmen than upon relations with kinswomen themselves: it is, after all, the wives of kinsmen that the patrilineage must depend on for its continuity rather than on its own women, who will eventually marry into other patrilineages. On the other hand, in *matrilineages intercourse with kinswomen would threaten the norms which provide for continuity of the kin group. *Bilateral systems, however, may treat both kinswomen and wives of kinsmen equally in terms of incestuous relations; both are involved in the continuity of the bilateral family and kinship groups.[9] Thus, in this explanation of the incest taboo, the fundamental problem in social organization is that of establishing conditions for permanence or change in patterns of social organization.

Certainly the study of social structure involves all three elements—psychological harmony, reciprocal relationships, and continuity. The question which the explanations of the incest taboo force upon us is: Which element is to be considered as basic for understanding how society works? In a relatively stable society, order and continuity are not problematic; instead, the description of the mechanisms used for maintaining psychological peace and reciprocal relations is important for understanding how the society is able to function. However, with rapid change in highly industrialized societies as well as in economically developing countries, problems of continuity and the maintenance of social order are most pressing. Hence, for the study of modern society, the explanation of the incest taboo as a device to permit continuity of family and kinship groups may be the most serviceable hypothesis—the one I shall apply in this analysis.

Implications embodied in incestuous-marriage prohibitions are central to the conception of family as property rights in related persons. There are two situations in which marital ties are not desirable. The first is one in which a kin group does not want to

⁹ Jack Goody, "A Comparative Approach to Incest and Adultery," *British Journal of Sociology* 7 (1956), pp. 286–305.

establish a cooperative relationship with another group. In American society, religious and racial intermarriage is often discouraged on this basis. The second situation for proscribing marriage is one in which individuals are already regarded as part of the same kin group. Marriage would then be superfluous in the creation of further alliances; the individuals are already closely related. In fact, marriage between members of the same closely related kin group may foster internal conflicts. Individuals in the range of relatives with whom marriage would be considered incestuous may be regarded as members of a person's *intimate-kin group,* which I discuss more fully in Chapter 2.[10] The intimate-kin group, whose membership is determined by incestuous-marriage prohibitions, simultaneously defines the outer limits of close familial relationships and the inner limits of marriageability.

As property, kinship refers partly to rules by which an individual inherits relatives, accrues them during his lifetime through birth or marriage, and transmits them to the succeeding generation. Continuity of a society over a series of generations demands stability in the kinship system in order to govern the succession of statuses and property rights. The composition of intimate-kin groups seems to reflect the manner in which the kinship system handles problems of social stratification and integration of family groups in the society.

MARRIAGE AND DESCENT

As I indicated in the preceding section, the biological aspects of sexual intercourse and birth provide the raw material for stabilizing and partitioning social relationships defined in terms of marriage and descent. In turn, the kin groups organized on the basis of marriage and descent provide the substance which integrates people into the larger social structure. Therefore, the topics of marriage and descent are central to understanding the ways in which social life is organized under different conditions.

In history, moreover, since family and household were the primal, undifferentiated collectivities from which specialized institutions later emerged, institutions such as government, industry, and the church, some insight into the nature of marriage and descent may yield knowledge about the basis for the persis-

[10] Bernard Farber, *Comparative Kinship Systems* (New York: John Wiley & Sons, Inc., 1968), pp. 14–21.

tence of society. Yet, inasmuch as both marriage and descent are involved in family organization, we must ask: Is marriage or descent more basic in the development and persistence of modern social structure? When various social scientists try to resolve this issue, they follow the paths of earlier writers who have considered the basic organizing principles of society.

In the social sciences, the issue of determining basic organizing principles has had a long history, one which can be traced back beyond the eighteenth-century Scottish moralists. The issue is evident in Adam Smith's two-fold basis for his analysis of society, i.e., his theory of moral sentiments and his model of the economy, the one founded on moral principles, the other on reciprocity. It is also apparent in the work of Adam Ferguson: writing in opposition to the Hobbesian position that society emerges as "the result of a bargain," Ferguson begins with the premises that (a) "families may be considered as the elementary forms of society" and (b) the parent-child relationship is the prototypical social bond. Children, and particularly infants, are helpless and "awake to every sentiment of tender concern, solicitude and love"; and the parents, for their part, "continue through life to seek the advantage of their child in preference to any interest of their own." The moral sentiments established in the interaction of parents and their children are extended and elaborated to produce consensus and loyalties which bind social groups (and possibly societies) into a cohesive whole.[11] At the same time, Ferguson does recognize the necessity for establishment of reciprocities to maintain order and continuity. In this sense self-interest merges with common interest.[12] Hence, for Ferguson (as for Smith), reciprocity parallels moral sentiment as a basis for society. In modern sociology, the dilemma of exchange versus morality remains unresolved. Some sociologists (like Gouldner)[13] attempt to reduce moral sentiments to a class of reciprocities; others (like Parsons)[14] see forms of exchange as an expression of more general sets of values. In the study of family

---

[11] Louis Schneider, *The Scottish Moralists on Human Nature and Society* (Chicago: University of Chicago Press, 1967), pp. 77–89.

[12] Ibid., pp. 211–219.

[13] Alvin W. Gouldner, *The Coming Crisis of Western Sociology* (New York: Basic Books, Inc., 1970), pp. 266–273.

[14] Talcott Parsons, "An Outline of the Social System," in *Theories of Society*, Talcott Parsons, Edward Shils, Kaspar C. Naegele, and Jesse R. Pitts, eds. (New York: The Free Press, 1961), Vol. 1, pp. 41–60.

and kinship, the problem of the priority of descent and marriage as organizing principles expresses the same issue.

Meyer Fortes, in assuming that kinship organization is derived from the requirement of the continuity of descent, emphasizes the moral principle of amity as characteristic of kinship and family norms in all societies; jural relationships, which tie family units to other institutions, are then based on mundane reciprocities.[15] Fortes thus sees *filiation, the creation of parent-child rights and obligations, as the fundamental relationship in family and kinship organization. Since it may be argued that family and kinship units are (in one form or another) universal and presumably the most basic groups in society, in this view moral principles are more important than reciprocities for the continuity of society.

To Claude Lévi-Strauss, however, marriage represents a transaction which may be basic to all other kinds of exchange in society. He assigns a central role to the prohibition of incestuous marriage in the development of systems of exchange; the proscription of marriage within prohibited degrees of kinship "tends to ensure the total and continuous circulation of the group's most important assets, its wives and daughters."[16] Kinship structures derive their form, according to Lévi-Strauss, from the ways they regulate marital exchange. If the form of marriage shapes the organization of kin groups, the nature of marital exchange in a society can be regarded as a prototype of general social structure. The study of the form of marital exchange, according to this view, reveals the structure of control over property. Insofar as the kin group is the repository of property in the society, this control extends also to all other forms of reciprocity, which become stabilized as institutional arrangements. Hence, for Lévi-Strauss, social structure obtains its form and endurance through exchange, and marriage is the "archetype" of exchange.

A third position—the one taken in this book—is to regard descent versus marriage (or the moral principle of amity versus the economic principle of reciprocity) as antithetical elements in structuring family and kinship units. This position implies that people are the property of their kinship units and can be either valued for themselves or used in exchange, depending upon the needs of the particular society. The dialectical position taken here

---

[15] Meyer Fortes, *Kinship and the Social Order* (Chicago: Aldine Publishing Company, 1969).

[16] Lévi-Strauss, *Elementary Structures of Kinship*, p. 479.

can be derived by refocusing statements made by Lévi-Strauss. To begin with, Lévi-Strauss contributed the insight that in marital transactions people represent a commodity essentially like all other goods (such as cattle, land, or tools). On the basis of this insight, analysis of kinship can stress either the accumulation of kin-group property over generations or its use in marital exchange. Lévi-Strauss has focused upon the latter usage. Yet the universal existence of limitations on marital exchange suggests another line of reasoning. The prohibition of incestuous marriage implies the presence of kin "groups" within which members cannot be exchanged for one another. The aggregation of these kin groups indicates that social structure can be defined in terms of nonreciprocities (as opposed to exchange). Generally, property can be viewed as something which may be withheld or prohibited from exchange. (For example, *entailed *estates cannot be sold.) In this regard, Lévi-Strauss[17] quotes Proudhon: "Property is non-reciprocity." Kin groups can vary in the amount and value of property they possess. Position in the social structure is determined not so much by the expenditure of kin-group assets in exchange, but by the ability of the kin group to withhold exchanges for its members until the right price is paid. In the final analysis, social position of a kin group seems to depend upon the extent of surplus value of assets over what is required for exchange in dealing with other kin groups. Seen in this light, social structure is molded by regulations which govern the accumulation, distribution, and transmission of kin-group property by inhibiting exchange and by dissipation of this property. In particular, persons within the range of prohibited marital relationships are the collective property of the same kin group, whose interests are to be maximized.

From the perspective of the opposing tensions of marriage versus descent in structuring family life, the nuclear family can be regarded analytically as a kinship unit in which the two forces are in balance. This *analytic* conception of the nuclear family differs from that expressed by Murdock, in which he views the nuclear family as an *empirically* identifiable unit in all societies.[18] Murdock holds that the nuclear family as an actual unit is able to perform a unique set of functions in all societies more effectively than any other institution. Parsons also accepts this position

---

[17]   Ibid., p. 490.

[18]   Murdock, *Social Structure.*

(although he has not decided just what "root" functions of the family are universal).[19] As an analytic concept, however, the nuclear family is a useful device for raising questions regarding the relative force of marriage versus descent (or reciprocity versus amity) in the maintenance of social structure. Although reciprocity and amity may both be significant in organizing social relationships, we still do not know which has greater weight in determining family and kinship organization at any particular time. The analysis in this book may offer some leads to the resolution of this issue.

MARRIAGE AND DESCENT IN INDUSTRIAL SOCIETIES

The conception of persons as kin-group property suggests that they are both (a) objects of value within their families of descent and (b) means for the creation of reciprocities through marriage. They are, as Lévi-Strauss[20] has proposed, at least in many preliterate societies, commodities by means of which kinship groups can engage in bartering. This view implies that many similarities exist between familial and economic institutions. If these similarities do exist, then we should be able to use the principles and major processes in one institution as a model for describing what happens in the other. Accordingly, concepts, propositions, and methods of analysis which have been developed for understanding the economy should be capable of being applied to family and kinship.

The following sections assume economic analogs to marriage and descent. They present propositions about changes in the use of persons as kin-group property in modern, industrial society. In explicating the emergence of new cultural models of family and kinship organization, succeeding chapters in the book will introduce elaborations and refinements of these propositions.

Marriage

All societies recognize some form of relationship which can be identified as "marriage." In this relationship, males and

---

[19] Talcott Parsons and Robert F. Bales, *Family, Socialization and Interaction Process* (New York: The Free Press, 1955), pp. 8–9.

[20] *Elementary Structures of Kinship.*

females are designated as having certain rights with regard to sex relations, household membership, rights with regard to their offspring, and rights and obligations pertaining to sustenance. From the viewpoint of perpetuation of kin-group property, marital exchange is a necessary evil unless it can be applied in such a way as to maintain or enhance family assets: (a) On the one hand, the family can perpetuate its property by requiring persons with preexisting consanguineal ties to marry one another (as in direct exchange of cousins) or to arrange marriages of relatives in a round-robin fashion (as in indirect exchange). (b) On the other hand, marital alliances can increase the usable assets of *both* previously unrelated kin groups involved in the marriages by giving each group simultaneous access to the other's resources.

Proposition 1

With industrialization and urbanization, the social organization of marital selection shifts from one of limited, segmented, specialized markets to more extensive market conditions whereby the diversity of potential marriage partners is increased. One can conceive of a bartering society at one extreme and national or international marketing areas at the other extreme. In the marital analog, bartering might be equivalent to prescribed *cross-cousin marriage; here the specificity in barter and cross-cousin marriage can be contrasted to the uncertainty in mate selection in modern western society. The presence of limited, specialized marriage markets creates a situation whereby the families have practically "total" knowledge about the field of eligible spouses. Often where this knowledge is not known to everyone participating in that market, the institution of the marriage broker may be developed. In the marriage market of modern western society, however, at best the potential spouses have a limited knowledge about their array of possible mates. Knowledge tends to be superficial at least at the beginning of courtship, and only after a long series of encounters is intimate information generally divulged. Even here, since much of the information comes from the person himself, knowledge about potential spouses is highly selective. In the movement from limited, specialized markets with total knowledge about potential spouses to extensive markets with limited knowledge, the character of marriage may be expected to change. In the former case, families can make permanent alliances with some certainty that they will be able to keep their bargains. In the latter instance, however, marital commitments must be tentative so that some fluidity may be maintained. In the extensive market, flexibility and liquidity would be maximized if each individual were to be considered as a potential spouse regardless of his current marital status. The sociological problem growing out of this market change is: How can continuity of the norms, values, and personal identities in a line of kinsmen be sustained with the shift from limited to extensive marriage markets?

Proposition 2

   In highly industrialized, urban societies, the primary mechanism in the marital market is the demand for potential spouses rather than their supply. In the extreme, ideal case, in a situation, that is, where any adult can be considered as a potential spouse regardless of his current marital status, the supply of eligible spouses can be regarded as infinite. What controls the marriage market then must be the demand by persons who regard themselves as being in a position to be married. The major problem for the supplying families is then one of marketing their children in marriages. Here the attractiveness of the "package" as well as the quality of the "product" itself may result in a successful marriage. Since his spouse is theoretically always available for marriage, the individual himself is motivated to remain prepared for the marriage market at any time; throughout his adulthood, therefore, he must prepare himself to remain marketable.
   One problem here is to determine how the supply and demand of spouses maintains an equilibrium. Because of the assumption that a person is eligible for entering a new marriage regardless of his current marital status, the supply of potential spouses in the population has some similarities to statistical sampling with replacement, in which being chosen in a sample does not preclude being chosen again. Hence, the pool from which persons are chosen is virtually infinite. The major problem in understanding the marriage market is that of demand: Why do people want to get married at all? Variations in the demand for spouses create an unstable market "price" in marriage.
   If the supply always exceeds the demand, and the market price is unstable, the bargaining power of kin groups is reduced. A large number of kin groups would have to be disappointed by their having to accept less desirable spouses. Hence there would be a tendency for the kin group to decline in its power over

individuals; it could not assure them of an acceptable, stable bargain.

In the process of the decline in power of kin groups over individuals, the value of stable marriage would necessarily diminish, and the role of filiation would tend to become stronger than marital bonds. "Lineage" would tend to replace the nuclear family as the basic kinship tie, while moral sentiments as organizing principles of family and kinship organization would tend to predominate.

Descent

If the economic analogy holds, the role of the descent group (whether nuclear family or kindred) is to create children who are highly valued in the society. It is motivated, therefore, to produce healthy children and to socialize them in ways which would maximize their worth and thereby permit the descent group to maintain or enhance its position in the society.

Many preliterate societies emphasize the ability of the corporate group to control and manage the daily lives of members. In these societies, the proprietorship of the descent group over members is aimed at maintaining its assets to insure its continuity over generations. Its control thus often emphasizes inhibition of deviance. With modernization, there is a greater tendency to take some risk in order to enhance the value of assets. In kinship, this enhancement would mean activities to increase the personal value of members of the kin group at the risk of producing neurotics or utter failures. The emphasis in modern societies then shifts from inhibitory control over members to investment in members. The investment in members consists of maximizing their ability to achieve a successful status in the society. The connotation of membership then shifts from that of fixed assets to assets of potentially increased value. In a sense, the membership group holds stock "certificates" (e.g., birth certificates showing legitimate offspring) of its members, the "price" of this stock being dependent upon the achievement of relatives. The role of kinship then changes from mundane control to sponsorship and facilitation of achievement. This leads to Proposition 3:

Proposition 3

In highly urbanized, industrialized societies, membership in descent "groups" entails a lesser degree of mundane management of conduct and a greater degree of investment in the individuals' welfare and in matters of policy regarding conduct. The shift in the role of descent groups from control to investment is related to the change in the conditions of the marriage market from segmented, specialized arrangements to markets of infinite supply of potential spouses. In the small specialized markets, individuals are to be tailor-made to fit the specifications of barter or of the demand of groups whose requirements are known. In the large market of infinite size, the particular desires of potential spouses and their families are not previously known, nor is the identity of future spouses even guessed at. Hence, rigorous control and discipline with regard to rights and obligations toward kin are then no longer necessary to insure the survival of the kin group. Instead, since probability of success may be high, the kindred can invest time, energy, and money in the development of individual members. However, in those segments of society where the probability of success is low (for example, families of low socioeconomic status), socialization of children here too may emphasize survival tactics rather than maximization of possible success in the society.

Proposition 4

The separation of ownership from control in kinship implies that in highly industrialized societies there tends to be a reduction of the rights and obligations of affines in familial relationships. If kinship is based mainly on investment in and promotion of the welfare of kin, the significance of relationships between affines would decline. Rather, people reserve their resources for their own relatives, who are permanent kinsmen. With a reduction of control by kindreds over conjugal families, the stability of marriage can not be ensured (particularly with the infinite supply of potential spouses with whom the son-in-law or daughter-in-law might replace his current spouse); the kin group may be pouring resources into a potentially bankrupt marriage. The decline in the significance of alliance between two kin groups removes the necessity of in-laws having some control over and interest in the spouses of their children. Hence the idea of a dual ownership (or partnership) whereby an individual belongs to two kin groups simultaneously is no longer a necessity. The rules governing the entire society might make membership in two *families of orientation (one's own and spouse's) an informal, preferential alternative rather than a legal arrangement.

Insofar as propositions borrowed from economists apply to family relationships, we can visualize a general cultural model which encompasses both family and economy with regard to norms and values. If this is truly an archetype of the entire culture, it should lend insight into other institutions as well. However, given the complexities of modern urban society, I have a hunch that such a gross model is more useful as a metaphor in cultural analysis than as a description of the general normative system of a society.

KINSHIP AND FAMILY LAW IN INDUSTRIALIZED SOCIETIES

Modern industrial society does not seem to function in terms of a single operating principle or paradigm which would be effective in organizing social relations uniformly throughout all segments of the population. One might think instead of a "core" and periphery, with the organizing principles working most effectively in the "core," i.e., in those segments of the population who serve as a reference point in the development of *civil codes. Take *divorce, for example. In pretwentieth-century England and in the early United States, divorce was possible principally through legislative enactment; the Parliament or legislature would enact a private bill providing for the divorce of a specific couple. Few divorces were obtained in this manner. For instance, in 1823 Georgia gave eight divorces, and in 1817 Louisiana granted three by legislation. This procedure could serve a limited "core" of the population in a society where an elite was seen as the only segment that counted politically and economically. But as the demand for divorce extended through the middle classes, divorce was turned over to the courts, with restrictions obtained through permitting divorce only for rigorous grounds and through making the legal process expensive. With further democratization as an operating principle of contemporary society, there is continuing pressure to facilitate divorce by easing the grounds and making divorce cheaper. In the past, those who have not been able to obtain a divorce have had to remain in a state of domestic misery or find other means for ending undesirable marriages. By looking at laws, then, we can see at least some of the guiding rules which organize family life at the "core" of society.

Laws regarding the family do not seem to develop haphazard-ly even in an industrialized society, but are instead the general expression of the kind of kinship organization which is prevalent among the dominant population. This kinship organization defines the way in which families are integrated into the social fabric. Since the structure of modern society is to a considerable extent the product of differential control over property (both productive and consumptive), "proprietorship" should loom large in our understanding of kinship.

The conception of kinship as property is apparent in legal terminology and definitions of rights and obligations. For example, the Napoleonic Code specifies conditions whereby a parent may *disown a child.[21] According to case notes in the *Annotated Laws of Massachusetts*, "Parents have no absolute right of property in their minor children of which they cannot be deprived without their consent."[22] Words such as surrendering, receiving, transferring, taking possession, renouncing are used in legal codes to refer both to persons (particularly children) and to their economic property. Indeed, many family laws appear to regard economic property as an extension of their owners. The Japanese Civil Code stipulates that "a person who exercises parental power manages the property of a child."[23] Seen in this light, the rights and obligations of support and succession derive from the proprietorship by family and kinship collectivities of relatives and their possessions.

Sections of legal codes dealing with basic kinship organization tend to persist over long periods of time, and to provide a context for legislation and court decisions to meet more immediate contingencies in the society. In particular, laws pertaining to incestuous marriage are generally stable from generation to generation. It is unlikely that most individuals are familiar with the specific laws governing incestuous marriage in their society. Yet these laws and their revisions do not represent random-like variations. They appear generally consistent with laws of guardianship, economic support, *illegitimacy, adoption, inheritance, and divorce. Together, they present a paradigm of family and kinship in the society which is indirectly conveyed to the members of the society.[24]

---

[21] Sections 312 and 313.

[22] 1969 edition, Ch. 210, Sec. 1, p. 358.

[23] 1962, Article 824, p. 165.

[24] Compare with Thomas Kuhn, *The Structure of Scientific Revolutions* (Chicago: University of Chicago Press, 1962), pp. 10–22.

When incestuous-marriage laws do undergo marked change, as they have in the past fifty years in England, this revision apparently signifies a profound modification of the social structure. With a change in legal codes pertaining to incestuous marriage (and, by implication, the kinship paradigm), other new laws relevant to husband-wife relationships, divorce, illegitimacy, support, adoption, and inheritance may be anticipated. These revisions invoke new images of ideal family organization and redefine which relatives an individual can regard as his own.

Changes taking place in European and American family law during the last century, illustrate the process of legal revision and modification of social structure. Much traditional family law in Western Europe distinguishes between "artificial" and "natural" nuclear-family relationships. The kinship model based on this distinction makes certain assumptions with regard to the relationship between family and state. According to this model, the natural, nuclear family derives its authorization or charter for existence from a source outside the state—in religion, in the mystique of blood relationships, in the maintenance of estates, or in other sources of traditional values.[25] Artificial family ties, in this context, are merely a creation of secular law and derive their legitimation from the state. *Statutory definitions of family rights and obligations are analogous to those pertaining to the natural family.

The distinction between natural and artificial family has various consequences for kinship relationships. One of these is that, by marriage or adoption, membership in "artificial" families of orientation may be *added* to a natural family. This cumulative aspect implies further that membership in families of orientation may be regarded as permanent, since one need not break off family ties to establish new ones. Membership in families of orientation may be overlapping.

The overlapping membership in two families of orientation seems significant when the extra-state charter of the natural family is also taken into account. Since the natural or ascriptive family derives its authorization for existence outside the state, the household may be regarded as extraterritorial government coming under state jurisdiction only insofar as it impedes or interferes with the normal life of the community. Transactions within families are thus private contracts. Under this conception, even

[25] David M. Schneider, *American Kinship* (Englewood Cliffs, N.J.: Prentice-Hall, 1968).

divorce (where it has no public consequences) could be settled as a private matter.

An alternative model emerging to replace the "natural" family is the conception of the family as a mere legal entity. In this model, since the only family relationships recognized are those in the law, the difference between natural and artificial family disappears. The state is then the only chartering agency for the legitimation of family relationships. An individual is not free to contract privately for particular rights and obligations associated with membership in another family; membership in families of orientation is not cumulative.

The noncumulative nature of membership in families of orientation according to the legal-family model itself has various consequences for kinship organization. The nature of affinal relationships is markedly different from that in the natural-family model. Whereas the natural-family model regards an in-law relationship as representing an actual family tie (creating obligations and rights by law rather than by natural relationship), the legal-family model does not. In the legal-family model, influences can carry moral weight in defining the personal ties among affinal relatives; but they have no legal standing. Since family ties are not cumulative in the legal-family model, marriage does not give an individual membership in his spouse's family of orientation: except as informal conventions based on religion or ethnicity may dictate, he has no duties or rights in that family of orientation. Conversely, the spouse's family of orientation can exert only informal controls over him.

Affinal proscriptions in incestuous marriage laws imply that upon marriag an individual becomes a member of his spouse's intimate-kin group. Specifically, if (as in *Levitical and *canon law proscriptions) he is forbidden to marry his parent-in-law following divorce or widowhood, marriage symbolically incorporates him into his spouse's family of orientation, and he thereby accrues a second family of orientation "artificially" by law.

Similarly, in adoption, the legal codes vary in providing for family membership. They may give an individual rights and obligations both in his natural family and in his adopting family; under these conditions, he would hold membership in both families of orientation. Alternatively, the adoption laws may require extinguishing membership in one family of orientation as a requisite for being adopted into another, and thereby limit membership to only one family of orientation.

PLAN OF THE BOOK

Three classes of family law seem to define changes that have occurred in modern industrial society. These classes include (a) laws regulating marriage, (b) rules of family membership, and (c) inheritance laws. Although these categories by no means exhaust all areas of family law, they do serve as indicators of the underlying paradigms guiding legislatures and courts in establishing the legal context of family life. Legal provisions regarding marriage, family membership, and inheritance are discussed in succeeding chapters.

Chapter 2 focuses on laws regulating marriage. During the past century, marriage laws have reflected a shift from limited marriage markets to an extensive market. To some extent, this shift is apparent in the increasing emphasis on freedom to marry found in the repeal of anti-*miscegenation laws and breach-of-promise legislation. Perhaps even more revealing of kinship organization are laws prohibiting incestuous marriage, which were discussed above. Analysis of trends in divorce law, divorce rates, and laws pertaining to incestuous marriage will suggest a shift in the kinship paradigms upon which family laws are based. The existence of a relationship between incestuous marriage laws and divorce is particularly relevant for Propositions 1 and 2. The analysis of legal impediments to marriage and divorce appears in Chapter 2.

Chapter 3 deals with the relative weight of marriage versus descent in the organization of the nuclear family. Changes in the rules of membership in laws which deal with support of family and kin, with adoption law, and with laws regarding illegitimacy are pertinent to Proposition 3, which stresses a decline of inhibiting control and an increase in investment in family members. Analysis of these laws will show whether the conception of "natural family," which has served in history as a basis for authority and control over family members, is declining as a legal concept. Shifts in adoption law are especially important for determining the status of the "natural family" in modern law. The treatment of illegitimacy again shows the possible significance of the "natural family" as a legal entity. Historical analysis of laws relating to support, adoption, and illegitimacy will thus indicate trends in the basic membership paradigms implicit in contemporary family law. Legal codes pertaining to family membership are discussed in Chapter 3.

Chapter 4 is concerned with descent. Proposition 4 indicates that in modern society emphasis is placed upon the development of assets and the increase of self-worth of descendants rather than on the minimization of risk to the nuclear family. The question faced in the establishment of inheritance laws is whose benefit is to be taken into account. Is the nuclear family the primary beneficiary in inheritance law or are lineal principles to be followed? The analysis in Chapter 4 is aimed at this problem.

In Chapter 5, attention is turned to the future. Here the American family will be examined more directly. The major questions dealt with in that chapter are: How have the historical changes in family law set the stage for what is to come? What kinds of family and kinship paradigms seem likely to guide the future norms of family life?

Finally, Chapter 6 summarizes the findings of the analysis and offers some conclusions. It will suggest that modifications of family in the future may be even more profound than those of the past.

2

Marriage and Divorce

The topics of marriage and divorce are so closely connected that the meaning of marriage in any society cannot be understood apart from the conditions under which divorce occurs. This chapter deals with paradigms of family and kinship implicit in modern marriage and divorce laws. Like the previous chapter, this chapter will emphasize the historical shift from the natural-family to the legal-family cultural model.

The natural-family paradigm postulates that the nuclear family exists as a universal, necessary entity in nature. Many social scientists, too, regard the nuclear family as the most efficient, stable social structure in nature for undertaking the functions which the family performs in society. Consequently, they have sought to find the basis for all familial norms in fulfilling these functions. In the natural-family conception, divorce implies the inability of husband and wife to carry out roles associated with the "natural" functions. The idea of divorce in the natural-family model thus indicates a failure of the family as an institution.

The conception of the family as a system of property rights, however, replaces necessity with utility as a basis of family organization. In economic terms, utility has the connotation of "using up" or consuming something. In family terms as well, one can "use up" a spouse and afterward replace him (or her). Divorce does not then denote failure of the family as an institution, but rather a need to replace personnel. The change in cultural models from the "natural" family to the "legal" family also represents, thus, a shift in the basis of family life from universal functions to utilization of personnel. The remainder of this chapter will be concerned with the relationship of social organization to marriage and divorce and with the increasing freedom of individuals to enter and leave marriages.

MARRIAGE AND SOCIAL ORGANIZATION: THE ROLE OF INTIMATE-KIN GROUPS

Chapter 1 defined intimate-kin groups as consisting of persons who were considered to be too closely related to marry one another. In modern societies, these intimate-kin groups are delimited in laws governing marital prohibitions pertaining to kinsmen. Statutes which prohibit marriages between relatives are usually headed as follows: "incestuous marriages," "what marriages are prohibited—consanguinity," "who shall not marry," "marriages void *ab initio*," "direct and collateral relatives—prohibited degrees," or "prohibited degrees of kindred and affinity." When the word *incestuous* is used, as it is in many statutes, it includes all relatives listed regardless of degree of relationship or whether they are affines or consanguineous kin. The term *incestuous marriage* is thus applied not only to nuclear-family members but also to more distant relatives.[1] This section of the discussion deals with the implications of first-cousin marriages and of affinal marital prohibitions for the changing social structure. It will relate the structure of intimate-kin groups to frequency of divorce, and it will indicate how the structure of intimate-kin groups is related to the ethos of industrial society.

First-Cousin and Affinal Proscriptions

In the United States, all states forbid marriage of nuclear-family members with one another and all include stepparents in their prohibitions. The greatest variations in marital prohibitions

[1] Bernard Farber, *Comparative Kinship Systems* (New York: John Wiley & Sons, Inc., 1968), pp. 25–28.

occur with regard to first cousins and affines. Of the 50 states (and the District of Columbia), 30 prohibit marriage between first cousins and 17 forbid certain affines (usually parents-in-law) from marrying. The view of kinsmen as property of the intimate-kin group raises questions regarding why different classes of relatives are covered by prohibitions of incestuous marriage. As the discussion which follows will show, those proscriptions pertaining to first cousins and affines are of particular interest.

In a variety of contexts, the permissibility of marriage between first cousins has been associated with marital stability. If kinsmen are viewed as property, and if *endogamy is regarded as a means for conserving property within the kindred, then consanguineous marriages (such as marriages between first cousins) may be regarded as a means for conserving the property within two families already closely allied through the siblinghood of parents.[2] Accordingly, as Ackerman[3] has found, the probability of divorce is low in bilateral societies permitting first cousins to marry. Similarly, Lévi-Strauss[4] has stressed the solidarity created between kin groups through prescriptive cross-cousin marriage.

In European and American kinship, the basis for affinal prohibitions is to be found in the Biblical conception of marriage. One commentator suggests:

> Starting with the foundation that by the union of man and wife they become "one flesh" the whole system of prohibited degrees laid down by Moses is simple and quite logical and coherent.

[2] In terms of the composition of intimate-kin groups, first-cousin marriage can be regarded as a means for creating even closer ties between related kin. Where marriage between first cousins is *forbidden*, *EGO's first-cousin's child cannot become a member of EGO's intimate-kin group by birth. With first-cousin marriage, however, EGO's cousin's child (who also happens to be EGO's child) *is* born as a member of EGO's intimate-kin group. In this way, first-cousin marriage acts to extend the ascriptive boundaries of the intimate-kin group to include the cousin's children. First-cousin marriage thus perpetuates close kinship bonds through several generations; if the first cousins who married had chosen different spouses, their respective children would have been second cousins to one another and their grandchildren third cousins.

[3] Charles Ackerman, "Affiliations: Structural Determinants of Differential Divorce Rates," *American Journal of Sociology* 69 (1963), pp. 13–20.

[4] Claude Lévi-Strauss, *The Elementary Structures of Kinship* (Boston: Beacon Press, 1969), pp. 98–145. See also Rodney Needham, *Structure and Sentiment* (Chicago: University of Chicago Press, 1962) and George C. Homans and David M. Schneider, *Marriage, Authority, and Final Causes: A Study of Unilateral Cross-Cousin Marriage* (New York: The Free Press, 1955) for an analysis of the controversy regarding the basis of the solidarity arising from cross-cousin marriage systems.

> Whomsoever of a man's own relatives he is forbidden
> to marry, the like relatives of his wife he is also forbidden to
> marry; he cannot marry his own sister, therefore he cannot
> marry his [deceased] wife's sister.[5]

The ban on marriages between affines has sometimes been
interpreted as an attempt to preclude competition, jealousy and
suspicion, and conflict between spouses of close relatives who
live nearby or in the same household.[6] However, laws are never
enacted prohibiting *unrelated* persons in the same or neighboring
households from marrying upon the divorce or death of spouses.
In fact, the Roman Catholic church recognizes living in the same
house as grounds for dispensation to permit close relatives to
marry.[7] Laws prohibiting marriage between affines thus apparently protect the unity of the intimate-kin group rather than the mere
tranquility of the household.

In safeguarding kinship ties, laws governing the prohibition
of marriage between affines are relevant primarily to the effects of
marriage on inheritance, authority, and obligations for assistance
of kinsmen regardless of residence. These laws imply that *kinship*
rights and obligations created by the marriage persist even after
the marital tie has been broken. The prohibition of marriage
between affines suggests that a family has an enduring obligation
toward men (or women) who marry its members; the inmarrying
persons are accorded a definite status which the family is supposed to maintain regardless of what happens to the marriage.

If relationships with spouses of relatives are considered to be
permanent, the kinship group then has a stake in the destiny of
the marriages of its members. It has an interest initially in the
choice of spouse and afterward in the quality of the marital
relationship. It is to the advantage of wealthy and powerful
families to choose carefully in selecting marriage partners for their
children. Afterward, it may seek tighter control over the marriage
and may supply assistance to the couple as part of its responsibility to maintain the community position of its members.
Sometimes circumstances do not permit the family to supervise or

---

[5]   George S. Holmested, "Marriage with a Deceased Wife's Sister," *Canadian Law Times* 25
(1905), p. 326.

[6]   Georges Ripert and Jean Boulanger, *Traite de droit civil d'apres le traite de planiol* (Paris:
Librarie Generale de Droit et de Jurisprudence, 1956), Vol. 1, p. 465.

[7]   H. A. Ayrinhac, *Marriage Legislation in the New Code of Canon Law,* rev. P. J. Lydon (New
York: Benziger Brothers, 1946), p. 378b.

control the marital relationships of its members; distance, poverty, or personal problems may interfere with family control. However, as an ideal, when community status is important, the ability of inmarrying persons to affect the future of the kinship group constrains the kindred to vest him (or her) with some rights of membership. Prohibition of marriage between affines hence seems to be associated with the maintenance of a stable, highly differentiated class structure in society. In contrast, permissibility to marry in-laws connotes an instability in affinal relationships. No assurance is given to families allied by marriage that their children are accorded any definite status in the families into which they have married. Intimate-kin groups are then under no obligation to stabilize marriages of their members.[8]

The function of affinal marital proscriptions in managing family property may be seen concretely in conjunction with Catholic law.[9] Canon law stipulates that marriage is a union of husband and wife in body and spirit; they are regarded as one being, irrevocably united. Essentially, each individual is incorporated symbolically into his spouse's family of orientation in the same status as his spouse.[10] Canon law restricts affinal relations to the spouse's blood relatives; EGO cannot marry his spouse's first cousin, but can marry this first cousin's spouse. The basis for introducing the impediment of marriage to affines in canon law is to scatter family ties in a broad network. Ayrinhac indicates that "the general reason for this impediment is to protect the morals of those who are thrown into close familiarity with each other, and to widen the range of human sympathy and love."[11] At the same time, "once affinity is contracted, it does not cease by the dissolution of the marriage which gave rise to it."[12] Conformity to canon law thus forces dispersion of the family by defining in similar fashion consanguineal *and* affinal ties in terms

[8] Bernard Farber, "Marriage Law, Kinship Paradigms, and Family Stability," in Clio Presvelou and Pierre de Bie, eds., *Images and Counterimages of Young Families* (Louvain, Belgium: International Scientific Commission on the Family, 1970), pp. 79–113.

[9] In canon law, marriage is proscribed between all consanguineal relatives in direct line of descendancy (and ascendancy), and collaterally the prohibition includes second cousins. However, the impediment to marriage to a second cousin is classified only as minor "and as such [is] rather easily dispensed" (T. Lincoln Bouscaren, Adam C. Ellis, and Francis N. North, *Canon Law, A Text and Commentary* [Milwaukee: Bruce Publishing Company, 1966], p. 557).

[10] Farber, *Comparative Kinship Systems*, pp. 49–57.

[11] Ayrinhac, *Marriage Legislation*, p. 179.

[12] Bouscaren, Ellis, and Korth, *Canon Law*, p. 86.

of both closeness of relationship and permanency. Affinal proscriptions thereby require *exogamy for gaining access to new
family property; the kindred must expand its field in seeking
resources. Whereas permissibility of first-cousin marriage is associated with stability of marriage when kinship *endogamy* is the
prevailing rule, affinal proscriptions seem indicative of stability
when marriages tend to be *exogamous*. Hence, both first-cousin
marriage and affinal marital proscriptions protect the integrity of
kin-group property; affinal prohibitions merely add another set of
relatives to be considered under conditions of kin-group exogamy.[13]

Intimate-Kin Groups and Divorce

As noted above, the extension of marital prohibitions to first
cousins and to persons already related by marriage seems to be
associated with the stability of marriage. A study by Ackerman[14]
has already shown that, in preliterate societies with bilateral
kinship systems, tendencies toward first-cousin marriage and
community endogamy are related to low prevalence of divorce.
Similarly, use of these principles of endogamy to maintain control
over individual members (and to thereby sustain a low divorce
rate) can be found in the Scottish clan and in other politically
defined units which effectively create limited marriage markets in
bilateral societies. The previous discussion suggested that in
modern societies not only permissibility of first-cousin marriage
but also prohibition of marriages between affines is connected
with a low divorce rate. This section will summarize a study of
the relationship between incestuous-marriage laws and divorce
rates, a detailed analysis of which has appeared elsewhere.[15] In
that analysis, data for four countries were compared: (a) the
United States, (b) England, (c) France, and (d) Sweden. Each
country expresses a different kind of kinship arrangement in law.
The United States provides a wide range of types of marital
prohibitions in its state legal codes. England illustrates a society
undergoing marked changes in laws pertaining to incestuous
marriage in 1960. In French society, the kinship paradigm implicit in the Napoleonic Code has changed little in the past 150

---

[13]   Farber, "Marriage Law, Kinship Paradigms, and Family Stability," pp. 92–94.

[14]   Ackerman, "Affiliations: Structural Determinants of Differential Divorce Rates."

[15]   Farber, "Marriage Law, Kinship Paradigms, and Family Stability."

years.[16] Sweden represents a legal tradition different from either English *common law or the French code. Marital proscriptions for England, France, Sweden, and the United States are summarized in Table 2–1. In the United States, each state has its own laws governing incestuous marriage. Two basic patterns of kinship organization implicit in the legal systems in the United States are indicated by marital prohibitions pertaining to first cousins and to affines. Those states which permit first-cousin marriage tend to prohibit marriage between certain affines, while states forbidding first-cousin marriage generally permit any affines to marry. The pattern of laws permitting first-cousin marriage but forbidding certain affines to marry appears mostly in New England and the southeastern states. It is an abridged Biblical system, based on Leviticus, but so pared that it resembles the kinship system implied in the modern English Marriage (Enabling) Law, 1960. The American pattern of laws prohibiting first-cousin marriage but permitting any affines to marry, however, is found primarily in midwestern and western states and is designated here as the western American system.[17]

For the most part, states that follow the pattern of various affinal prohibitions but first-cousin permission (an attenuated Biblical model) originated as English colonies, whereas states permitting any affinal marriage but prohibiting first-cousin marriage tend to be those settled later as part of the vast western frontier (the western American model). At one time in American history, the attenuated Biblical model was relatively more prevalent than it is today. Some states, such as Illinois in the nineteenth century and Delaware in the early twentieth, switched from an attenuated Biblical model to the western American model. Other states like Pennsylvania and Texas have changed their laws piecemeal by adding first-cousin prohibitions or by dropping affinal proscriptions. Still other states, like Iowa, still seem to follow an attenuated Biblical model in statutes but have invalidated laws pertaining to affinal marriage through court action.[18]

---

[16] See Max Rheinstein, "The Code and the Family," in Bernard Schwartz, ed., *The Code Napoleon and the Common-Law World* (New York: New York University Press, 1956), pp. 139–161.

[17] Farber, *Comparative Kinship Systems*, pp. 25–45.

[18] Ibid.; Frank J. Indovina and John E. Dalton, *Statutes of All States and Territories with Annotations on Marriage, Annulment, Divorce (with Cumulative Supplement)* (Santa Monica: Law Publishing Company, 1945 and 1956); and Frank H. Keezer, *A Treatise on the Law of Marriage and Divorce* (Indianapolis: Bobbs Merrill, 1923).

TABLE 2–1 RELATIVES WITH WHOM MARRIAGE IS FORBIDDEN BY LAW IN VARIOUS NATIONS

Nations	Direct Descendants and Ascendants		Brothers and Sisters		First Cousins		Uncles and Aunts	
	Consanguines	Affines	Consanguines	Affines	Consanguines	Affines	Consanguines	Affines
England (before 1960)	X	X	X	X			X	X
England (Marriage Enabling Act, 1960)	X	X	X				X	
Sweden	X	X	X				X¹	
France	X	X	X	X			X¹	
United States[2] Western American pattern	X		X		X		X	
Biblical-based pattern	X	X	X				X	

¹Also includes Great-uncles and Great-aunts
²Thirty-four of the fifty states (and the District of Columbia) conform generally to either the western American or Biblical-based (derived from Leviticus primarily) patterns.
  Source: Bernard Farber, "Marriage Law, Kinship Paradigms, and Family Stability," in *Images and Counterimages of Young Families*, Clio Presvelou and Pierre de Bie, eds. (Louvain, Belgium: International Scientific Commission on the Family, 1970), pp. 96–113.

Although all countries in Table 2–1 forbid marriage with members of the nuclear family, they vary with regard to other relatives. France and Sweden prohibit marriage with great-uncles and great-aunts, but the United States and England limit avuncular marital proscriptions to uncles and aunts. All kinship paradigms analyzed, except for western American kinship, permit first-cousin marriage. As for affines, the French and traditional English paradigms include collateral relatives of the spouse in marital prohibitions; Swedish, modern English, and American-Biblical paradigms include only direct-line ascendants and descendants; the western American paradigm makes no provision for affinal restrictions on marriage. The most prominent historical tendency in laws pertaining to marriage between relatives has been to reduce affinal proscriptions; other aspects of incestuous-marriage law are generally stable. Presumably, as noted earlier in the discussion of exogamy, the more affinal kin included in the intimate-kin group, the lower is the probability of divorce.

In a comparison of divorce rates over a sixteen-year period (1950–1965) in Table 2–2 for France, England (and Wales), Sweden, and the United States, the following trends in divorce per 1000 married women occurred, consistent with discussion of intimate-kin groups:

1. Until the 1960's, England had a lower divorce rate than France; in the 1960's, however, England's divorce rate approached that of France.

2. In the United States, those states in which marriage between specified affines is forbidden tended to have a lower divorce rate than states in which all affines are permitted to marry.

3. With the western American kinship system as the most prevalent paradigm in the United States, the American divorce rates were consistently higher than the English or French rates.

4. Swedish divorce rates were lower than the American rates but higher than the English and French rates.[19]

In addition, in these countries the average duration of marriage prior to divorce is associated inversely with the rate of divorce. Where high divorce rates exist, people tend to choose divorce as an alternative solution to marital problems sooner.[20]

The findings lend plausibility to the interpretation that the kinship paradigms which are implied in laws pertaining to incestuous marriage do influence family stability. To some extent,

[19]   Farber, "Marriage Law, Kinship Paradigms, and Family Stability."

[20]   Ibid.

TABLE 2-2 DIVORCE RATE PER 1000 MARRIED WOMEN FOR
FRANCE, ENGLAND AND WALES, THE UNITED STATES,
AND SWEDEN, 1950-1960

	France	England and Wales	United States	Sweden
Year	Divorce Rate	Divorce Rate	Divorce Rate	Divorce Rate
1950	3.59	2.75	10.32	4.92
1951	3.39	2.54	10.03	5.12
1952	3.25	2.97	10.18	4.91
1953	2.97	2.64	9.93	4.99
1954	3.01	2.42	9.55	5.05
1955	3.09	2.29	9.39	5.12
1956	3.07	2.23	9.44	4.97
1957	3.00	2.00	9.28	5.06
1958	3.03	1.89	9.20	4.91
1959	2.87	2.02	9.40	4.93
1960	2.86	1.96	9.22	5.01
1961	3.07	2.10	9.62	4.83
1962	2.84	2.34	9.41	4.87
1963	2.75	2.58	9.64	4.64
1964	2.98	2.82	10.05	4.95
1965	3.09	3.04	10.64	5.10
1966			10.79	5.43

Sources of data: Central Statistical Office, *Annual Abstract of Statistics*, No.
104, 1967. London, Her Majesty's Stationery Office, p. 14. Also No 99, 1962–1963,
p. 13; No 97–98, 1960–1962, p. 14.
Great Britain Registrar General, *Statistical Review of England and Wales*,
1955. London, Her Majesty's Stationary Office, 1957, p. 5. Also, 1957, p. 5; 1955,
p. 4; 1956, p. 4; 1954, p. 10; 1964, p. 4; 1965, p. 5; 1951, p. 4; 1952, p. 4.
Statistical Office of the United Nations, *Demographic Yearbook*, 1967, 19th
issue, Dept. of Economic and Social Affairs, United Nations, New York, 1968, pp.
758–760. Also 17th issue, 1966, pp. 796–799; 14th issue, 1962, pp. 606–609; 11th
issue, 1959, pp. 632–635.
U.S. Bureau of the Census, *Statistical Abstract of the United States*, 1968,
(89th edition). Washington, D.C., 1968, p. 32. Also 1967 (88th edition), p. 33; 1966
(87th edition), p. 31; 1965 (86th edition), p. 31; 1964 (85th edition), p. 31; 1963
(84th edition), p. 36; 1962 (83rd edition), p. 37; 1951–1960 (82nd edition), 1961, p.
35; 1951 (72nd edition), 1951, p. 24.
Ministère de l'Economie et des Finances, *Annuaire Statistique de la France*,
Institut National de la Statistique et des Etudes Economiques, Vol. 73, 1967, p.
32. Also Vol. 70, 1964, p. 24; Vol. 69, 1963, p. 10; Vol. 68, 1962, p. 9; Vol. 67, 1961,
p. 13; Vol. 64, 1958, p. 7; Vol. 63, 1957, p. 5; Vol. 62, 1956, p. 5; Vol. 61, 1955, p. 7;
Vol. 60, 1954, p. 10; Vol. 59, 1953, p. 10.
Ministère des Finances et des Affaires Economiques, *Statistique du Mouve-
ment de la Population*, Institut National de la Statistique et des Etudes Economiques, 1950–51, Presses Universitaires de France, Vol. 25–26, 1956, p. 23, 25. Also
1946–49, Vol. 23–24, 1953, p. 35, 37.
Suereges Officiella Statistik, *Fölkmängdens Forandringar*, Statistiska Cen-
tralbyran, Stockholm, 1967, p. 19.
Suereges Officiella Statistik, *Bufolkningsrörelsen*, Ar. 1960, Statistiska Cen-
tralbyran, Stockholm, 1962, p. 10. Also, 1961, p. 10, 1960, p. 10; 1959, p. 13; 1958,
p. 13; 1957, p. 13; 1956, p. 42; 1955, p. 42; 1954, p. 42; 1953, p. 10, 1952, p. 10.
Source of table: Bernard Farber, "Marriage Law, Kinship Paradigms, and
Family Stability," in *Images and Counterimages of Young Families*, Clio Presvelou and Pierre de Bie, eds. (Louvain, Belgium: International Scientific
Commission on the Family, 1970), pp. 88–89.

the data fit Ackerman's hypothesis that bilateral societies which permit first-cousin marriage will have lower divorce rates than those fostering kinship-group exogamy by forbidding first cousins to marry.[21] In the four societies examined in this chapter, the Ackerman hypothesis would account for the high American divorce rate as compared with the European rates (as well as for differences between states). It would not explain, however, (a) the rise in the English divorce rate in the 1960's without a revision in laws permitting first-cousin marriage, (b) canon law restrictions on both divorce and first- and second-cousin marriage, or (c) Sweden's divorce rate being higher than that of the two other European countries (since all permit first-cousin marriage).

In large measure, the findings do reflect changes in incestuous-marriage law involving affined in *collateral* relationships in modern societies, where exogamy is the rule. In contrast, laws governing incestuous marriage of direct-line ascendants and descendants (or those of the spouse) have remained intact in modern law. When France instituted its Civil Code, it eliminated the more extensive restrictions on marriages between collateral kin in canon law, but retained some affinal as well as consanguineal proscriptions pertaining to lineal relatives. In the United States the retention of remnants of Biblical kinship has also been restricted mainly to lineal affines. The changes in England during the twentieth century have been similar. Likewise, the Swedish kinship paradigm relies heavily on lineal ties—in sharp contrast to canon law. The reduction of lateral extensions in the intimate-kin group, particularly with regard to affines, seems to indicate a continual weakening of its proprietory rights in managing its members in exogamous marriages.[22]

Intimate-Kin Groups in Industrial Society

In general, the inclusion of affines in the range of relatives with whom marriage is prohibited implies, as we have seen, that ties based on marriage are permanent and that the larger kinship groups—including the parental families of the married couple—have a stake in selecting spouses for their children and in maintaining the marriage. Families at high socioeconomic levels

---

[21] Ackerman, "Affiliations: Structural Determinants of Differential Divorce Rates," p. 16.

[22] See Jacob W. F. Sundberg, "Marriage or No Marriage: The Directives for the Revision of Swedish Family Law," *International and Comparative Law Quarterly* 20 (1971), pp. 223–238.

in particular would have an interest in the ability of their children's marriages to sustain the "family" status in the community. Indeed, in those countries with extensive affinal prohibitions on marriage the divorce rate tends to be low, and prevalence of divorce is greater at lower socioeconomic levels of the society.[23] Restrictions on marriage between persons already related through marriage thus seem to be associated with the maintenance of a hierarchial social structure. The direction of change in incestuous-marriage laws is to limit affinal prohibitions; this shift suggests basic changes taking place in modern social structure toward democratization.

In industrial societies sundry processes go on simultaneously which change fundamental property relationships connected with kinship. Hunter[24] suggests that modernization consists partly of a shift in orientation from one aimed at conserving existing assets (i.e., minimizing risks) to one directed at maximizing assets. In Western, nonsocialist industrial societies like the United States, maximization of economic assets, accompanied by a sharing of risk, has led to the invention and proliferation of stock companies. Most productive property is controlled by stock companies; without the creation of the stock company, capitalism might indeed have been seriously impeded in its development. As a stock company, the "corporation" is a legal fiction established to identify a particular collective enterprise. Since business enterprises exceed kin groups in scope, ownership of productive property is then not the exclusive province of a *single* kin group; rather, assets of a stock company are generally apportioned among numerous unrelated families. Transactions with regard to productive property in modern society pertain, then, to buying or selling stocks, i.e., gaining access to resources (but not management) in a collective enterprise. Property takes on the connotation of using resources without exclusive control by any single owner (or kin group) over their allocation.

Insofar as norms and values pertinent to kinship conform to the general conception of property in a society, the modern kindred may be viewed as a fictitious entity (like the corporate stock company) which maximizes its assets, in part, by deriving the benefits from the property of other kin groups. Marital alliances consequently involve, not the *transfer* of members to

---

[23] William J. Goode, "Marital Satisfaction and Instability: A Cross-Cultural Analysis of Divorce Rates," *International Social Science Journal* 14 (1962), pp. 507–526.

[24] Guy Hunter, *Modernizing Peasant Societies* (New York: Oxford University Press, 1969).

affinal kin groups, but a mutual utilization of property rights. In lieu of transferring relatives from one group to another, marriage gives kin groups *access* to each other's resources. In this situation, relatives and family connections may still be valuable kinship property, with socioeconomic position (as an expression of the worth of assets) determining the kinds of sharing accomplished by marriage.

Hence, if the analogy between economic and familial property holds in modern society, changes in the prevailing conception of property would be reflected in revisions in the composition of the intimate-kin group, as defined by legal codes, through the reduction of affinal proscriptions. The modifications in the general paradigm of property rights in modern society seem to reflect the continual increase in size and complexity of corporate enterprises. Applied to kinship, these changes signify a continual decline in control over kin-group members and a concomitant extension of the potential marriage market for any individual.

THE FREEDOM TO MARRY

The natural-family model implies that, since affinal ties are permanent, there should be firm control by parents over their children's marriages. From the viewpoint of marital stability and of the prospective spouse's life chances, this control requires clear criteria for defining a desirable spouse. Since *ascriptive characteristics provide the best guesses that parents can make about prospects of possible sons- and daughters-in-law, these achieve some importance as criteria in their choice (or support of their child's choice). Hence, attributes of race, religion, ethnic background, legitimacy, reputation of family, socioeconomic background of family, and family's wealth and power all may influence the marital decision. It is feasible for persons to have extensive knowledge about these attributes only in a limited marriage market.

With the reduction of parental control over marriage of their children, however, criteria associated with limited marriage markets dissipate. Courtship and engagement change in significance with the enlargement of marriage markets and the decline of the parental role. Consequently, the legal safeguards that had been considered as necessary to protect the "natural" family from "bad" marriages are no longer appropriate. Court decisions and legislation are aimed instead at increasing personal freedom to marry.

Modifications in laws governing the freedom to marry reflect the changing conception of marriage in America. This section is concerned with those actions which have abolished two kinds of restraints on marriage: laws forbidding interracial marriage and laws relating to breach of promise to marry. Interracial-marriage laws deal specifically with an ascriptive characteristic (differences of race) generally associated with life chances in American society; these laws also have their roots in such myths as racial superiority. As for laws relating to breach of promise action, they have had a long history in Europe and America; their abolition represents a significant change in the concept of engagement or betrothal as well as in the legal conception of the courtship process.

Racial-Intermarriage Laws

Throughout American history, there has been strong pressure to inhibit racial intermarriage, particularly between blacks and whites. During the nineteenth century, laws directed against miscegenation were passed in all sections of the country. Although there was some relaxation of these prohibitions immediately after the Civil War in states such as Mississippi, this action was only temporary. As of 1960, twenty-nine states—a majority of the United States—had laws prohibiting interracial marriage. These states forbade marriages of whites to blacks, Chinese, and Japanese, as well as to Filipinos. While California placed no barriers on marriages of Mexicans or American Indians, other states did prohibit marriages with American Indians. In the sixties, under the doctrine of equality before the law (as provided by the Fourteenth Amendment to the U.S. Constitution), states swiftly removed barriers to interracial and interethnic marriages. By 1967, only sixteen states retained statutes prohibiting racial intermarriage. In June 1967, however, the U.S. Supreme Court in *Loving v. Virginia* firmly established the basic norm that ethnic or racial background cannot be made a condition for marriage. The *Loving* decision constitutes a recognition that ascribed status, based on ancestry, is not a legitimate barrier to marriage, and it signifies the demise of limited marriage markets confined to specific ethnic and racial groups.

Anti-miscegenation laws were intended to sustain the nineteenth-century social order consistent with the natural-family

cultural model, which posits a set of "natural" functions in the
nuclear family as necessary to uphold the general values and
norms of the society. The specific goals and rules of conduct
pertaining to family life would then have to conform to the needs
of the larger society. In order to enforce conformity to these
norms, the state had to curb impetuous and capricious behavior of
family members, who might marry nonconformists or otherwise
socially or "biologically" undesirable persons. The state, along
with the church, therefore imposed various impediments to a
marriage which might endanger the future of society. Statutory
restrictions, in addition to consanguinity and affinity, have included minority of age, nonresidence, mental incompetence,
venereal disease, delays for premarital examination, and waiting
periods for the remarriage of divorced persons. Indeed, the
discouragement of irresponsible or incompetent persons from
marrying has "constituted almost the only purpose behind the
vast array of statutes specifying which persons may marry and
when."[25] If the law is intended to help people "to resist . . .
impetuous and importunate inclinations, . . . any number of
mandatory barriers to marriage can be justified."[26]

If, however, marriage is regarded in the category of "vital
personal rights" or "basic civil rights of man," as the U.S.
Supreme Court has suggested, the functions of the family for the
larger society and the need for marital restrictions are irrelevant.
The act of marriage itself has then replaced the particular form of
marriage and family life as a "natural" phenomenon. It follows
that what is done or how things are done in any particular family
are matters of private and not public—or legal—concern. The
institution of marriage thereby achieves a right to exist apart from
the content of marital interaction or of the kinship networks
created by it. This situation opens the way for a wide differentiation of styles of family life in the society.

Breach of Promise to Marry

The increasing number of alternatives open to families influences the ways in which relationships between men and
women develop. As long as the "natural family" remained as the

---

[25] Robert F. Drinan, "The *Loving* Decision and the Freedom to Marry," *Ohio State Law
Journal* 29 (1968), p. 376.

[26] Ibid., p. 379.

dominant cultural model, becoming engaged implied a promise to follow the norms expressed in that model. With a multiplicity of acceptable life styles, however, each engaged couple must work out its own destiny.

In contemporary American society, people become engaged and break off engagements with ease. They regard the act of engagement as a statement of intention to marry and view the engagement period as a time for testing aspects of their relationship. Ending an engagement is thus seen as having few long-run consequences for the man or woman. The *intention* to marry is in no way a *promise* to marry.

The perception of engagement as an intention to marry differs considerably from that implied by betrothal. In betrothal, the act of engagement is a promise to marry, and it assumes that all arrangements associated with marriage are contractual. Given that interpretation, breaking of the contract to marry could have dire effects. On the basis of an exchange of promises to marry, a couple might act in ways which, if no marriage took place, could prove especially harmful to the woman. There might be a large expenditure of funds in preparing for the wedding, a dowry might be given, a virgin might consent to sex relations, the woman might give up other opportunities for marriage, or she might give up her job or career. In some societies, the breaking of a betrothal can alienate families irrevocably.

The conception of betrothal as a contract seems to have come initially from early German custom and to have influenced American law through English common law and French practices.[27] Damages for breach of promise to marry were awarded in ecclesiastical courts as far back as the thirteenth century. Originally, a brideprice was paid to the bride's guardian at the time of betrothal and was not refundable. Later, the bridegroom merely promised at the betrothal to pay upon marriage; but even if he refused to go through with the marriage, his obligation nevertheless remained. With the passage of time, the financial obligations gave way to personal and symbolic duties upon betrothal. Yet, the possibility of a court action for damages persisted for the "defence of morals and protection of the bride" into the twentieth century.[28] The first American law prohibiting court action for breach of contract to marry came in 1935 in

---

[27]   Paul Weidenbaum, "Breach of Promise in Private International Law," *New York University Law Quarterly Review* 14 (1937), p. 462.

[28]   Ibid.

Indiana. Afterwards, there was a flurry of similar legislation in other states, particularly in those with large urban populations— New York, Pennsylvania, California, Illinois, New Jersey, and Massachusetts, among others.

Public opinion regarding legislation outlawing breach of promise suits emphasized the abuses resulting from these court actions.[29] Women were no longer dependent beings whose very destinies hinged upon the marriage contract: they did not suffer irreparable damage from a broken engagement; but the possibility of court action encouraged the pretense of heartbreak (when in fact the woman might have manipulated the whole affair). The betrothal had changed in significance.

The newer meaning of the engagement period is also suggested by the fact that the "anti-heart balm" legislation, which eliminated breach of promise suits, often did away with court action for the alienation of affection of a married person. The ability to bring suit for alienation of affection was regarded as a protection against "marauders who wantonly attack the family relationship."[30] The previous permissibility of breach of promise and alienation of affection suits had implied that the woman, whose role in the "natural" division of labor in the family left her defenseless, required financial redress. These actions were also intended to be punitive against the destroyer of marital promises. They were thus meant to protect the sanctity of the family in performing its "natural" functions—procreation, regulation of sex relations, socialization of children, and economic maintenance. Their abolition was a sign of the weakening of the natural-family model as a guiding principle in law.

The trend away from engagement and marriage as contractual arrangements and toward their definitions as *personal* relationships implies a gradual elimination of differences between married and unmarried status. The blurring of these differences has important consequences for marital relationships. Writing about family law in Sweden, one observer has remarked, "In a society in which you can entertain sexual relations with almost everybody, impediments to marriage begin to look ridiculous."[31] In such a situation, even current marital status might not be considered to be a serious bar to becoming engaged to—that is,

---

[29] James P. Byrnes, "The Illinois Anti-Heart Balm Law," *Illinois Law Review* 38 (1943–1944), pp. 94–99.

[30] Ibid., p. 99.

[31] Sundberg, "Marriage or No Marriage," p. 231.

intending to marry—another person. The languishing of the natural-family model as a basis for marriage law carries with it the emergence of the view that courtship, engagement, and marriage signify degrees of personal commitment rather than contractual arrangements. As functionalist anthropologists and sociologists have often pointed out, personal commitments are fragile, and a social order based only on personal commitment is tenuous.

DIVORCE AND SOCIAL ORGANIZATION: HOUSEHOLD COMPOSITION AND MALE-FEMALE RELATIONSHIPS

The above sections on marriage have indicated ways in which changes in laws regarding impediments to marriage express the decline of the natural-family model as a guiding principle for family norms in the United States. The gradual elimination of restrictions on marriage between affines, the prohibition of first-cousin marriage, and the abolition of antimiscegenation laws and breach of promise actions—all these suggest an increasing freedom to marry almost anyone in the society. Once people come together in marriage, however, another set of forces comes into being—the living arrangements associated with domestic life. In the final analysis, the stability of marriages depends upon these arrangements.

If we assume that in any society some couples will be unable to get along and will want to end their marriage, we can ask: How do norms governing domestic arrangements facilitate or hinder divorce among couples who desire to separate? To what extent do living arrangements constrain couples to stay together? Two kinds of domestic norms that seem particularly important in assessing the probability of divorce in a society are (a) those governing authority relationships between men and women and (b) those connected with the composition of the household.

The first domestic factor, the relative dominance of husband versus wife in marriage, is related to the divorce rate. Those societies in which the husband has authority over the wife tend to have a lower divorce rate than those in which equalitarian norms hold in marriage.[32] In these societies, pressures are applied not only by the husband but also by the wife's relatives to keep the

---

[32] Max Gluckman, *Custom and Conflict in Africa* (London: Basil Blackwell, Ltd., 1956), pp. 54–80.

marriage intact. Provided that the husband does not exceed norms of brutality, he finds support throughout the community for his control over his wife. Where equalitarian norms hold, however, forces which bind the subordinate person to a marriage dissipate; he or she is no longer required to submit to demands which might be considered unreasonable. The justifications of the family division of labor which call for subordination as "natural" no longer apply. Consequently, the familial constraints which hold the woman in a subordinate position can no longer be maintained, and divorce must be available if she cannot abide by the marital relationship.

The second factor, household composition, is significant in divorce especially when there are children. Since there are two parents, divorce brings up the question: To whom do the children belong, the mother or the father? How shall they be disposed of? In many societies divorce may have a traumatic effect on the children, and parents may inhibit their desire to end the marriage because of its possible consequences for the children. In other societies, however, the household is so constituted that marital breakup requires only minimal changes in the children's upbringing. Here divorce does not threaten the children's welfare, and parents are not constrained to uphold an unhappy marriage.

This section will deal with norms of household composition and male-female relationships as elements affecting divorce in widely diverse societies. Social scientists frequently assume that preliterate or traditional societies (especially those organized into patrilineages) have low divorce rates. However, traditional societies with high divorce rates effectively illustrate the roles of household composition and male-female relationships as factors in the divorce rate.

Household Composition

What happens to a household upon divorce of a couple? In modern American society it usually breaks up, and the children live with their mother. Often the mother must go to work, and the whole household routine is consequently disrupted. The lives of the children may be altered drastically.[33] Yet in some societies the

---

[33] After an initial period of distress, children may find their home life more bearable than it was prior to the divorce. Research evidence is that in the long run children whose parents have been divorced seem no worse off emotionally than those whose parents continue to endure an unhappy marriage. Yet, divorce may imply a whole series of adaptations, especially for boys.

stability of the household does not depend on the presence of a married couple. The composition of the household may be such that it can continue to exist through generations without stable marriages. Given this condition, wives may cease to be a valuable commodity, and divorces may be prevalent. The Kanuri people of northeastern Nigeria, a feudal society organized patrilineally, with an unusually high divorce rate, provides an example.[34]

Kanuri marriage is polygynous, and half the men have more than one wife at a time. Almost all Kanuri women can look forward to taking turns in the care of the husband and sharing the burdens of the household. The woman is isolated from her husband's kin and must be constantly on the alert to avoid conversation especially with her father-in-law. The seclusion of women facilitates male dominance.

Depending upon the location in a village or urban center, 68 to 99 percent of Kanuri marriages end in divorce. Most divorces occur within the first four years of marriage. The major reasons given for divorce are female insubordination, and inadequacy of performance of roles by men and women. The higher the socioeconomic status of the husband, the higher the rate of divorce, and urban residence is associated with the tendency toward divorce; however, the fertility of the wife and age of the man are negatively related to marital breakup. Among the Kanuri, divorce does not always require legal proceedings. As in other Moslem societies, the man may merely say, "I divorce you" before witnesses, or he may send a letter if the woman is living elsewhere. Women call upon the courts to initiate a divorce.

The high divorce and remarriage rates among the Kanuri are possible because of the presence of a patrilineal household compound, which is the basic unit of Kanuri social and political organization.[35] Household units are linked together through the kinship ties of their male heads into larger political groupings.

Although a mother's employment may not in general produce harmful effects on the personality development of children, the combination of the divorce crisis, father absence, and maternal employment could provide an unusually stressful situation. See James Walters and Nick Stinnett, "Parent-Child Relationships: A Decade Review of Research," *Journal of Marriage and the Family* 33 (February, 1971), pp. 82–83; Harold L. Wilensky, "Women's Work: Economic Growth, Ideology, Structure," *Industrial Relations* 7 (May 1968), p. 243; and F. Ivan Nye and Lois W. Hoffman, eds., *The Employed Mother in America* (Chicago: Rand McNally & Company, 1963), pp. 67–212.

[34]   Ronald Cohen, "Brittle Marriage as a Stable System: The Kanuri Case," in Paul Bohannan, ed., *Divorce and After* (Garden City, New York: Doubleday, 1970), pp. 182–212.

[35]   Ibid., p. 205.

When a Kanuri "thinks of his 'home' he thinks of the household he was raised in—not the family—for, in general, the family breaks up in a few years."[36] In divorce the woman moves out and leaves her children; the children are then raised by one of the father's other wives, or by one of his sisters.

The Nayar represent the matrilineal analog to the Kanuri households. Nayar women and their brothers live in an extended household. Although the women are married ritually, the husband does not have exclusive sexual or residential rights in his wife. According to Gough's[37] description, "a woman customarily [has] a small but not a fixed number of husbands from within her neighborhood," and although relationships with these husbands can be of long standing, the woman is also permitted to receive casual male visitors "of appropriate sub-caste who [pass] through her neighborhood in the course of military operations." A regular husband within the neighborhood has some obligations—to present his wife with gifts and to provide the fee for the midwife. There are no permanent links with the husbands' kin, however, and relationships between men and their wives and children are generally fragile.

The Kanuri and the Nayar represent extreme cases where the stability of the household is independent of the tenure of husbands and wives in a household. In neither case does the endurance of the household, with its task of socializing of children, depend upon the maintenance of the husband-wife relationship. The constant presence of women in the household, regardless of their marital status, makes possible family continuity despite high marital turnover.

In Western society, domestic life has been organized as a household unit in ways which inhibit divorce. The natural-family model presupposes that each nuclear family lives in an independent household. This supposition is derived from the position that the functions which define the nuclear family pertain only to the relationships between parents and their children. If the unique system of functions, such as sexual regulation and socialization, is considered as necessary and sufficient to define the family, the family must then be restricted to the group (that is, parents and children) that performs this configuration of functions. To maintain its boundaries in perform-

---

36 Ibid., p. 206.

37 Kathleen E. Gough, "The Nayars and the Definition of Marriage," *Journal of the Royal Anthropological Institute* 89 (1959), pp. 23–34.

ing these functions, the family must exist as a distinct household unit.

But if the nuclear family exists as a distinct household unit, both parents must be present in the home to fulfill their roles in order to enable the family to perform its functions properly. For this to occur, their marriage must remain intact. Hence, the natural-family paradigm presupposes that the nuclear family resides in an independent household and that the parents' marital bond is permanent. The model therefore supports the position that those family forms which rely upon the presence of the married couple to maintain a stable household dictate against divorce. It is likely that among population segments with a high divorce rate in American society, households frequently contain adults other than the parents; studies of lower-class families in particular show the presence of persons outside the nuclear family.

Male-Female Relationships

Another factor which seems important in the divorce rate is the kind of authority relationship existing between men and women. Generally, a high status of women is associated with a high divorce rate. Status, however, is not the only important factor, as the case of the Kanuri above suggests. Yet, among both "primitive" and modern peoples, the relative status of men and women is of some importance in the propensity to divorce. The Bakweri, a Bantu-speaking people in the Cameroons, provide an example.

The divorce rate is high among the Bakweri. The Bakweri are patrilineal, although there are some obligations established with matrilineal kin. In previous generations the divorce rate had been low but is now reaching high proportions. Of all legitimate unions ever contracted by women, forty-two percent end in divorce or separation. This high rate of divorce seems inimical to the general expectation that divorce rate is low in patrilineal societies.[38] Among the Bakweri, as is common in patrilineal groups, the children belong to the father's kin, and the children of divorced parents remain with the father's people. The findings on divorce, however, indicate that by far the most unstable marriage is that with a junior wife in a polygynous marriage. In such a situation,

---

[38]   Gluckman, *Custom and Conflict in Africa*, p. 70.

the senior wife (or other co-wives) remains in the household to care for the children.

A clue to the trend toward higher divorce for the Bakweri is the changing status of women. One woman, aged about fifty, indicated that "old marriages were stable as women obeyed husbands . . . in the old days when a person did not obey her husband she was beaten."[39] According to another elderly woman, "When we were young we had hard lives but were loyal. Now there is plenty of money which attracts the young ones about. Marriages were respected in our youth. Now sons-in-law can say anything in front of us, eat in our presence [taboos broken]. If your daughter commits an offense against her husband, and he asks you for a reconciliation, she will not accept, but want divorce."[40] In previous generations, it would appear that parental control of women was a significant factor in keeping marriages together. Another old widow says, "If I was married in the old days, maintained [by my husband] or not, my parents would have made me stay married."[41] The role of parents in the past was described by a middle-aged woman: "Previously if a woman married a man and there was a dispute, the father would beat her if she was wrong, and that made marriages firm." That the changing status of women is a factor in divorce is suggested also by the large proportion of divorces obtained because of ill treatment by the husband, including beating, correcting the wife in public, destruction of her property, quarreling, and drunkenness or crime. Next to property maintenance, ill treatment is the major reason given by women for divorce. Among the patrilineal Bakweri, like the Kanuri, the nature of the household (which may include several mature women), the institution of polygyny, and the increased autonomy of women may all stimulate divorce.

With industrialization, numerous changes in male-female authority relationships have occurred in European and American society. In a cross-cultural analysis of nuclear-family organization, Morris Zelditch[42] has found that, as in experimental small

---

[39] Edwin Ardener, *Divorce and Fertility, An African Study* (London: Oxford University Press, 1962), p. 94.

[40] Ibid., p. 93.

[41] Ibid., p. 94.

[42] Morris Zelditch, Jr., "Role Differentiation in the Nuclear Family: A Comparative Study," in Talcott Parsons and Robert F. Bales, *Family, Socialization and Interaction Process* (New York: Free Press, 1955), pp. 307–351.

groups, families in practically all cultures tend to have a task leader and an expressive leader. In the family, the husband is almost always the task (or instrumental) leader and the wife the expressive (or social-emotional) leader. One might imply from this finding that these roles have their basis in "nature," in the childbearing and childrearing roles of the mother and the status-providing and economic roles of the father. Yet, if one no longer accepts these sexual domains as natural, then the authority relationship growing out of this "natural" division of labor can no longer be justified.

Zelditch suggests that one possible exception to tendencies in his findings is the "American middle-class case." But even here he indicates that although both husband and wife can participate in childrearing, housekeeping, and outside employment, *normatively* there are still sexual domains. Had Zelditch chosen Sweden in his sample, he might have reached a different conclusion. According to Tomasson,[43] there are more occupational opportunities, particularly at professional levels, available to Swedish than American women. These permit Swedish women to regard an occupational career as a primary commitment, and their home life as secondary. Maternity leaves, birth grants, postnatal health care, child allowances, and late marriage facilitate occupational commitment of women. "The assumption . . . that the provider is male and the dependent is female has certainly been destroyed" in Swedish conceptions of the family.[44] Given this view of the status of women in society, the familial division of labor must be revised, and it is not surprising that Sweden has eased its grounds for divorce.

THE FREEDOM TO DIVORCE

This chapter so far has suggested that the freedom to marry is associated with a decreased emphasis on relationships with affines and with a decline in the role of parents in mate selection. It has also indicated that increase in divorce rates has its roots in the decline of the nuclear-family household as an ideal and in the changing status of women. Together, the characteristics of family

[43] Richard F. Tomasson, "Why Has American Fertility Been So High?" in Bernard Farber, ed., *Kinship and Family Organization* (New York: John Wiley & Sons, Inc., 1966), pp. 327–338.

[44] Sundberg, "Marriage or No Marriage," p. 224.

life revealed by all of these changes point to elements comprising the legal-family cultural model which has evolved in contemporary society. This section, on the growing freedom to divorce, will further clarify distinctions between the natural-family and legal-family paradigms.

In the natural-family cultural model, divorce is a dire step. Since the natural family as a set of norms obtains its charter outside the law, matters pertaining to marriage and divorce must be viewed in relation to their extra legal purposes. In the natural-family paradigm, divorce law is intended to sustain "natural" rights (which are derived from the "natural" functions of the family). The legal-family paradigm, however, is based only on a legal charter, and divorce law must rely only on the purpose of the marriage intended by the spouses. Hence, in the natural-family paradigm, marriage and divorce are *means* to an end, whereas in the legal-family paradigm, they are *ends* in themselves.

Common-law systems of Western Europe and the United States have traditionally utilized the concept of "grounds for divorce," in which one party accuses the other of violating rules of "decency" or of being incompetent to carry out the *purposes* of the marriage.[45] The emphasis in these laws is more upon the extralegal ends of marriage to maintain a perpetual line of "natural" families than upon marriage as a personal relationship between husband and wife. Divorce is generally permitted only if the injured spouse can show that the violation makes impossible the continuation of the "natural" family. Generally, traditional grounds for divorce include acts which interfere with carrying out the duties of spouse or parent, such as adultery, cruelty, impotence, mental incompetence, incarceration, habitual drunkenness, and desertion. Since the purpose of marriage is to create a "natural" family for children, acts which are grounds for divorce interfere with the maintenance of "natural"-family obligations. For each divorce ground, fault is assigned to one spouse for his or her failure to carry out marital or parental obligations. Divorce is then viewed as a form of recrimination by the wronged spouse (as well as by "society"), so that the spouse at fault cannot continue to benefit from the marriage and to exploit his mate (and "society") without carrying out his own duties. Failure to carry out marital and familial obligations is, therefore, defined as a threat to the maintenance of a perpetual line of "natural" families and consequently to the fabric of society itself.

[45] See Max Rheinstein, "Divorce and Law in Germany: A Review," *American Journal of Sociology* 65 (March, 1960), pp. 489–498.

The legal-family conception, however, pertains only to the maintenance of the particular family relationships themselves. The purposes of the marriage, as personal matters, are irrelevant to the legal maintenance of the husband-wife relationship. In this conception, the reason for the breakdown of the marriage is less important than the fact of the disintegration of the marital relationship. The family is no longer a "natural" entity in this conception but only a legal fiction; and moral or religious foundations are considered private matters and irrelevant to the legal form of marriage and the family. The law is not intended to sustain any particular set of moral and religious prescriptions. Therefore, laws based on the legal-family conception do not require that fault be assigned to one spouse for failing to carry out his marital and familial duties. The "natural" right of family and the recrimination in divorce give way to the conception of the breakdown of a marital relationship as a legally valid cause for divorce.

The different grounds for divorce under the natural and the legal conceptions of family carry with them corresponding presuppositions about marital relationships which pertain to the nature of marriage contracts. The idea of recrimination and of the adversary system in divorce procedures suggests a situation whereby someone has not lived up to the provisions of a contract. The divorce law is viewed as condemning particular conduct, which constitutes grounds for breaking the marriage contract. It is held by those who oppose marital breakdown as a ground that "if the law enabled [a guilty spouse] to divorce without any difficulty, it would be equivalent to approval, not condemnation, of his blameworthy behavior. It would give rise not only to moral repulsion, but also to concern for the impact of law on the human mind, since the law which does not condemn, but approves blameworthy behavior, demoralizes the community instead of educating it."[46] From the perspective of marital alliances, then, divorce for reprehensible behavior constitutes a remedy for breach of contract at the expense of a breakdown of the network of relationships which binds the society together. This contract was established at the beginning of the marriage.

The conception of marriage as a binding contract, for which "prices" or benefits and obligations are fixed at the time of the wedding, provides a contrast to the conception of marriage as a *relationship* formed by two people who are at the same time

---

[46] Jan Gorecki, *Divorce in Poland* (The Hague: Mouton, 1970), p. 124.

merely continuing members of their own natal families. The latter view does not conceive of marriage as formed by a single contract, but rather as a constant negotiation of rights and obligations extending throughout the couple's lifetime. The perennial renegotiation of rights and obligations in the relationship is inherent in the concept of "marital breakdown." The breakdown of a marriage is in effect the result of the inability of a couple to continue to renegotiate acceptable arrangements.

Stated in another way, the view that marriage is created by a single contract at its inception implies that at the wedding an individual undergoes a major change in status, one which is often associated with creation of obligations not only to his spouse but also to affines. This change in status would in general be symbolized (at least legally or jurally) by membership in the spouse's intimate-kin group after marriage. However, where marriage is seen as a series of contracts constantly under renegotiation as conditions change, entering marriage should not itself invoke a profound modification in status. Rather, the changes in status may occur perhaps imperceptibly as rights and obligations are negotiated continually by the married couple, who retain their basic kinship identity in their families of orientation.

Of course one would expect that recriminative divorce law does not by itself affect the divorce rate significantly. Finland may be used as an example:

> In Finland the breakdown of marriage is one of several grounds for divorce, among others being the widely accepted grounds of adultery, cruelty, desertion. Until 1948 the rule of recrimination was enforced in Finland: in a case in which the breakdown of marriage was a ground for divorce, the predominantly guilty spouse was prevented from claiming divorce. This rule was discarded in 1948. However, its cessation, in the years 1948–1957, did not result in any significant rise in the divorce rate, in any significant shifts in the number of petitions on the grounds of breakdown of marriage or on other grounds: these data suggest, that at least in Finland, the rule of recrimination was not an effective motivation for human behavior.[47]

Rather, we would expect that other grounds would be used for obtaining a divorce even where the couples themselves thought in

[47] Ibid., p. 116.

terms of the breakdown of the marriage. When consulted about
divorce, even lawyers may question the couple from the perspective of marital breakdown—seeking to determine whether reconciliation is possible—but then proceed on the basis of whatever
legal grounds seem feasible.

The conception of marriage as a relationship in which rights
and obligations are constantly under negotiation further implies
that divorce, instead of merely ending a marriage, is a continuation of this relationship under different conditions. The conception of divorce as an ongoing relationship is apparent particularly
when there are children. If the children are in the mother's
custody, the father must constantly negotiate rights and obligations regarding visitation. In receiving child support (in addition
to alimony), the mother is also obliged to maintain the relationship with her ex-husband. Bohannan remarks:

> The relationship between ex-husband and ex-wife is poorly
> charted in American culture. When remarriage of one or both
> of the ex-spouses creates new husband-wife relationships, it
> simultaneously creates the possiblity of extended affinal
> relationships: the two women who stand to one another in a
> relationship of husband's ex-wife to ex-husband's wife;
> another relationship of the two men who are wife's ex-
> husband and ex-wife's husband to one another. And if both
> these relationships are present, as they are at remarriage of
> both partners to the original marriage, the even more ex-
> tended relationship of ex-husband's wife's ex-husband to the
> ex-wife's husband's ex-wife.[48]

Bohannan also suggests that it is not unusual for the former
spouses of the two new spouses to know one another. The
network of relationships is complicated further by the presence of
children. The children then may have two or more sets of parents.
Their stepparents are not so much substitute parents as they are
supplementary parents. Given this pattern of in-law relationships
and step-relationships, a complex network of affinal kin is established without extinguishing the existence of earlier consanguineal relationships.

In summary, the grounds for divorce under the legal-family
paradigm imply different presuppositions about husband-wife

---

[48] Paul Bohannan, "Some Thoughts on Divorce Reform," in Bohannan, ed., *Divorce and
After,* p. 118.

relationships than do the grounds consistent with the natural-family paradigm. The adversary system in divorce procedures and its concomitant basis of divorce as a form of recrimination assume that husband-wife interaction is based on a stable set of norms on which there is considerable consensus throughout the community. Consequently, the original marriage contract constitutes an agreement to abide by these norms. These norms draw their stability and consensus from the supposition that the purpose of marriage is extralegal and is founded upon "natural" law. In that conception, marriage exists to perpetuate natural-family lines. Performance of acts which break the contract therefore threatens the social fabric, and recrimination is thus inherent in the conception of divorce. In contrast, the legal-family paradigm implies that the purposes of marriage are private and therefore not based on community consensus or on stability. It suggests further that the conditions for the marriage contract may change over the family life cycle, with the married couple undergoing a continual renegotiation of rights and duties. When the couple cannot come to an agreement in renegotiating conditions for maintaining their marriage, the marriage can be said to have broken down, and divorce exists as a solution without recrimination. In any meaning of divorce, however, the relationship between the ex-husband and ex-wife must go on because of necessary arrangements which continue to be negotiated with regard to children resulting from the marriage. Apart from this, the natural-family and the legal-family paradigms thus have significant implications for conceptions of husband-wife relationships and the marriage contract.

CONCLUSION

This chapter has discussed paradigms of kinship organization implicit in marriage and divorce laws. Starting with the premise that family membership is a form of property right, it has explored variations in the meaning of marriage and divorce in modern societies.

Divorce law in particular reveals assumptions made about the nature of marriage in a society. In the natural-family paradigm, the adversary system in divorce procedures and the conception of divorce as a form of recrimination assume that husband-wife interaction is based on a stable set of norms on which there is considerable consensus throughout the community. The marriage vows constitute a contract to abide by these norms. The persistence of these divorce laws over generations derives from the supposition that the family and marriage draw their charter from "natural" law. Acts which are grounds for breaking the marriage contract threaten the "natural" social fabric, and recrimination is thereby inherent in the conception of divorce. The legal-family paradigm, however, implies that the purpose of marriage is private and therefore without any basis in an enduring community consensus or stability. Based on private understandings, a marriage undergoes continual renegotiation as the conditions of domestic life change. When this renegotiation fails, the marriage is regarded by the participants and by the court to have broken down, and the couple can divorce without assigning fault.

The historical trend toward the legal-family paradigm can be interpreted as a shift away from regarding the family as a "natural, " objective entity whose structure is molded by its social functions in regulating sex and socialization. The legal-family paradigm, which posits *private* motivations for forming and maintaining marriages, presupposes a considerable amount of variation in the norms of family life which people actually follow. The legal-family paradigm thus seems appropriate in a society with extensive marriage markets, requiring a tolerance for diverse norms.

The diffusion of the legal-family cultural model in Western Europe as well as in the United States suggests that the changing meaning of marriage is not merely a national phenomenon but is instead related to the general democratization of modern, industrial society. As long as the natural-family paradigm played a prominent role in society, social-class designations could split communities into small demes, which were homogeneous with regard to ethnic, religious, or cultural attributes. The limited marriage markets served to maintain the existing social strata in the society. According to the legal-family model, however, all styles of family life are equivalent provided they are based on monogamy. There is, therefore, no restriction to impede anyone from marrying anyone else. It follows that courtship and marriage cannot be restricted by categories of ethnicity, age of the participants, socioeconomic characteristics, or any other social-class designations. All adults in the society have equal rights before the law, and, so far as the state is concerned, are included in the same system of courtship and marriage.

With democratization extending equal rights to *all* adults, distinctions between married and unmarried status are minimized. Consequently, the contractual aspects of engagement and marriage, which make explicit the duties associated with engagement and marital status, decline in importance; people tend to view them as mere formalities. But 'if engagement and marriage are perceived, not as a contract but as a statement of intention to live together and to love and to cherish until death, no adult can be held to his intentions. And, since married versus unmarried status is minimized, adults cannot be barred from participating in other courtships—and engagements—because of current marital status. But if courtship and engagement of married persons is permitted, then the state is obligated to end undesirable unions so that desirable ones can be created. "Unprofitable" or bankrupt marriages (as the saying goes) may be ended, and profitable ones established. Any individual is thus permanently available for marriage with anyone else (presumably of the opposite sex) without regard to current marital status.

3

Support, Illegitimacy,
and Adoption

Basic rights and obligations of family membership are embodied in laws pertaining variously to support of indigent kin, status of illegitimate children, and the consequences of adoption. Some statutes have stressed lineal descent, and others, the nuclear family as the fundamental bond in kinship.

Legal emphasis upon descent is at variance with the usual assumption in sociological studies that the basic domestic unit in *all* societies consists of a nuclear-family configuration of father, mother, sons, and daughters. Bronislaw Malinowski regarded parenthood as the source from which the nuclear family arises as the basic kinship unit. For him, "the role of sociological father, that is guardian and protector, [is]the male link between the child and the rest of the community." He considered the father as "necessary for the full legal status of the family."[1] Aside from this role Malinowski held that the child is linked to both parents "by the unity of the household and by the intimacy of daily contact. In most communities both parents have to look after it, to nurse it,

[1] Bronislaw Malinowski, "Parenthood—the Basis of Social Structure," in *Sourcebook in Marriage and the Family,* 2d ed., Marvin B. Sussman, ed. (Boston: Houghton Mifflin, 1963), p. 44.

and to tend it." In his view, the family gives the child access to the resources of the kinship group as he matures into adulthood.

In defining the nuclear family as the basic unit in social organization, Malinowski perceived that the relationship between family and kinship group is in some ways antagonistic. On the one hand, "the direct growth of the family is helped by the local grouping of households by cooperation within the neighborhood, by the fact that, for many purposes, the relatives of both father and mother are relevant to the child." On the other hand, "the splitting and breaking up of the family on the unilateral principle and the correlated building up of clan ties is achieved gradually in some communities by the teaching of the rules of descent and the introduction into tribal condition and ritual, or dramatically in others by initiation, by esoteric clan ceremonial and mystery performances, and by the rules of clan exogamy and classificatory terminologies and institutions."[2] He believed that the "legal figment of exclusive kinship in the one line, that is of clanship, is never fully adjusted to and balanced with the claims of the family." He thus regarded the family and the kinship group as two functionally distinct entities and considered the larger kinship unit as "essentially non-reproductive, non-sexual, and non-parental."[3]

Functionalists like Malinowski believe that the characteristics of kinship organization are a product of the male and female relationships within the family. Their reasoning is as follows:

1. The basis for social differentiation lies in sexual division of labor. Some ecological circumstances make the man predominant in economic matters; others make the woman predominant; still others give men and women equal predominance. Predominance in economic relationships is associated with power and control within the family.

2. Where the economic role of men is predominant, *residence of the newly married couple tends to be with or near the husband's parents; where women are predominant, residence is matrilocal; where both husband and wife are of equal importance, they choose their residence for idiosyncratic reasons, often near the more powerful or more wealthy set of parents.

3. Residence tends to involve property ownership as well as

---

[2] Ibid., pp. 45–46.

[3] Unlike Lévi-Strauss, Malinowski regarded marriage as a crisis which is necessary for parenthood but which places strain on social relationships. Lévi-Strauss, however, views marriage as a basis for stable social structure.

control over the destiny of the married couple's family. Consequently, residence rules tend to give rise to rules regulating descent. Matrilocal residence generally leads to matrilinearity; patrilocal residence to patrilinearity; neolocal residence to bilaterality.

4. Descent and residence rules determine the kinship terminology applied in the society.

Despite the reasonableness of Malinowski's position, there is no logical necessity for starting with sex-role differentiation in economic matters in order to explain family and kinship organization. An investigator could start with the problem of kinship structure rather than functions of the nuclear family. He could study the creation of rules of succession in order to indicate how these rules place limits on sexual division of labor, rules of residence, variations in descent, and kinship terminology. Indeed, some studies have indicated what the influence of inheritance practices is on kinship organization. Goody investigated the consequences of passing on property through women as well as through men and suggested that bisexual inheritance seems to encourage such tendencies as (a) prohibitions on premarital sex relations among women, (b) monogamy, (c) marriage with father's brother's daughter, (d) kinship terminologies that differentiate siblings from cousins, and (e) provision of alternatives among bilocal, neolocal, and virilocal residence upon marriage.[4] Thus, to start with ecological variables is arbitrary and not logically necessary. Starting with succession of office or of property rights, the researcher would emphasize not so much the nuclear family (e.g., starting with economic functions and sex differentiation) as he would the larger descent group, the corporate entity or conglomerate that controls members and things as its property.

In assuming the crucial role of the nuclear family, Malinowski did not weigh the relative importance of the father (a) in his own right as guardian of the child or (b) in his capacity to represent the larger kinship entity. Perhaps Malinowski considered that since descent, succession, and inheritance can take place on the mother's side in some societies, sociological fatherhood must be assumed to reside within the nuclear family itself. In matrilineal kinship, however, guardianship and protection is often afforded by the mother's brother, and men obtain sons and heirs by offering their sisters as wives in the creation of a network

---

[4] Jack Goody, "Inheritance, Property, and Marriage in Africa and Eurasia," *Sociology* 3 (January 1969), pp. 55–76.

of alliances in which these same men receive the women of other kin groups. Consequently, in contrast to Malinowski's emphasis upon the father, Robin Fox suggests that "problems of paternity need not trouble matrilineal societies. It matters little who the father is—a man is his mother's child and this fixes his status. . . . Logically, marriage is only a marginal institution in matrilineal society."[5] Thus, for Fox, the source of legitimacy and guardianship is the larger kinship group rather than the nuclear family. In this context, it is *descent* rather than nuclear family which is the more fundamental relationship in the maintenance of social structure.

The problem of determining which is more fundamental is probably insoluable. Judging from the continual argument between the structuralists and functionalists, it is probable that empirical demonstration of either explanation is impossible at this time. Perhaps the most effective way of handling the problem is to see the extent to which trends in modern law favor nuclear family as opposed to descent as alternative principles of organizing norms governing kinship. Particularly relevant to the study of these principles are situations which are abnormal with regard to family membership. (a) For example, in the normal nuclear family, parents are obligated to support their children. Which of the two principles does the law apply in handling the dependency of persons other than children? (b) Or, to cite another example, in the normal family the children are legitimate and consequently have certain rights of support and inheritance. What happens to these rights when the child is illegitimate? (c) Or, in still another case, the children in normal families are the biological products of procreation. Which principle guides enactment of laws of adoption of children? The analysis of laws of support, illegitimacy, and adoption from a sociological perspective may reveal shifting trends in the application of nuclear-family and descent principles in regulating family life. Hence, this chapter will examine state laws pertaining to obligations to support relatives, rights and duties of illegitimate children, and the status of adopted children.

SUPPORT OF RELATIVES

In every society, parents or their representatives are obligated to maintain children until the children become self-supporting. Some societies have rituals of adulthood attached to this in-

---

[5] Robin Fox, *Kinship and Marriage* (Baltimore: Penguin Books, 1967), p. 115.

dependence; others rely on other signs to indicate the self-sufficiency of the child. The roles may eventually reverse, with the parents dependent upon the child. But, saying that a child *ought* to support his destitute or dependent parents may express a nicety instead of a prescription. If this obligation is merely preferential, then there are no laws requiring such support and no formal sanctions applied for failure to provide parental support. If, however, to support parents is considered essential to the general welfare, laws are passed and children face punishment for failure to abide by them.

Enactment of laws prescribing support for dependent adults by their families apparently reflects the seriousness with which states view this obligation. Moreover, extending this prescription to cover relatives besides parents suggests that lawmakers (and influential pressure groups) must apply some principles of family and kinship organization to determine who should be included. That being the case, a review of state codes regarding obligations for support outside the nuclear family may reveal the relative strength of nuclear family and descent in defining family and kinship organization obligations in modern society.

English common law did not obligate a child to support an indigent parent.[6] Instead, the child's first duty being to his own children, one's *family of procreation took precedence over his family of orientation. It was not until 1601 that an English statute created the duty of the child to provide support for his parent. Some American colonial laws then extended support duties to the grandparental generation, thereby breaking down further the nuclear-family boundaries implied in common law. For example, Massachusetts passed a law in 1692, reenacted in 1788 and again in 1793, which provided for the following:

> The kindred of such poor persons, in the line or degree of father or grandfather, mother or grandmother, children or grandchildren by consanguinity, living in the Commonwealth, and of sufficient ability shall be bound to support such poor persons in proportion to their respective ability.[7]

Later, Massachusetts (as well as Connecticut) dropped its provisions for supporting indigent grandparents. However, this

[6] "Recent Cases," *Minnesota Law Review* 23 (January 1939), p.243.

[7] Cited in Stefan A. Riesenfeld, *Modern Social Legislation* (Brooklyn: Foundation Press, 1950), p. 699.

revision does not seem to represent a trend in that New Hampshire and Rhode Island, whose earlier laws included only parents,
later added obligations to grandparents in their laws governing
support.[8]

The laws of the fifty states (and the District of Columbia)
regarding obligations to support relatives who cannot support
themselves fall into several patterns:

1. Sixteen of the states do not have any such laws and
therefore rely either on custom or on governmental agencies to
provide support. Generally, they are "common law" states. For
the most part, these states are in the southeast region (Florida,
Kentucky, Mississippi, North Carolina, and Tennessee) or in the
southwest (Arizona, Arkansas, Kansas, Missouri, New Mexico,
Nevada, Oklahoma, and Texas). Only Vermont, Washington, and
Wyoming lie outside of these southern regions. Perhaps the
absence of harsh winters precludes the need to enact laws
requiring support of relatives.

2. In twenty-one states, obligation to support needy relatives
is restricted to children's duty to their parents. These laws
provide a reciprocal to the earlier obligation of parents to support
their minor children. States which restrict support obligations to
children's responsibility for their parents are not limited to any
particular region. These states seem to follow the old English
statute.

3. The third pattern of statutes pertaining to support obligations places the responsibility not only on children to take care of
their parents but also upon grandchildren to support their needy
grandparents. The states which adhere to this pattern are widely
scattered (District of Columbia, Iowa, Maine, Louisiana, New
Hampshire, Rhode Island, and New Jersey). Clearly this pattern
emphasizes lineal descent.

4. The fourth pattern obligates an individual to provide
support for members of his immediate family—his parents, his
brothers, and his sisters. This pattern omits obligations to grandparents. Only two states conform to this pattern (Illinois and West
Virginia).

5. The final pattern, in which an individual is obligated to
support parents, grandparents, and brothers and sisters, displays
both nuclear-family and lineal-descent tendencies. Seven states
fall into this pattern (Alabama, Alaska, Colorado, Minnesota,
Montana, Nebraska, and Utah).[9]

[8] See Connecticut statutes, 1866, Chapter 4, Section 40, Notes.

[9] Alabama requires brothers but not sisters to support needy siblings.

With the many revisions in support and pauper law, there is no clear indication to suggest trends to restrict obligations to the immediate family or to emphasize lineal descent. However, the trend away from common law and toward the civil code tradition implies an increase in emphasis on descent; this trend is illustrated in the German Civil Code of 1896, which stipulates:

1. Lineality has priority over collaterality.
2. Descendants are obligated before ascendants and collateral kin.
3. Closer ascendants are called upon before the more remote ones. (Kin are obligated to provide support in order of *intestate succession.)
4. Ascendants of equal degree are obligated in equal parts.
5. The spouse of a needy person is liable for support before other relatives.[10]

The German Civil Code of 1896 suggests a connection between laws of intestate succession and support laws, a connection which implies in turn an underlying coherence of general kinship rights and obligations. "The modern tendency [is] to recognize the duty of support as pointing out the line of inheritance . . . . This trend also appears in the increased inheritance rights granted between an adopted child and his foster parents, and the tendency to cut off rights of inheritance from the natural parents. The analogy lies in the fact that, by adoption, the child's natural parents are relieved of their duty of support while that duty is imposed upon the adopting parents."[11] The kinship paradigm suggested by the German Civil Code emphasizes lineality and refers to members of the nuclear family (except for the spouse) in terms of their *kinship* ties rather than special *family* obligations. In contrast, the English law of support, rooted in the Biblical kinship paradigm, stresses nuclear-family rights and duties as distinct from extrafamily kinship obligations.

It is noteworthy that for income tax purposes, the United States Internal Revenue Service appears to follow the natural-family paradigm in determining qualification of relatives as dependents. Persons who qualify as dependents, although they may reside in a separate household, include certain affines and all blood relatives within the third degree of relationship:

[10] Max Rheinstein, "Motivation of Intergenerational Behavior by Norms of Law," in *Social Structure and the Family*, Ethel Shanas and Gordon F. Streib, eds. (Englewood Cliffs, N.J.: Prentice-Hall, Inc., 1965), pp.252–254.

[11] Marilyn Klosty and Harold J. Weiss, "Editorial Notes: Illegitimacy," *Brooklyn Law Review* 26 (1959), pp. 72–73.

Your child, grandchild, or great grandchild, etc. (a legally adopted child is considered your child);

Your stepchild, but not the stepchild's descendants;

Your brother, sister, half brother, half sister, stepbrother, or stepsister;

Your parent, grandparent, or other direct ancestor, but not foster parent;

Your stepfather or stepmother;

A brother or sister of your father or mother;

A son or daughter of your brother or sister;

Your father-in-law, mother-in-law, son-in-law, daughter-in-law, brother-in-law, or sister-in-law.

Once any of the above relationships [has] been established by marriage, [it] will not be terminated by death or divorce.[12]

ILLEGITIMACY

As in laws pertaining to support, illegitimacy laws seem to reflect the underlying kinship paradigm prevalent in a society. Like support laws, those pertaining to illegitimacy cover abnormal contingencies. In effect, they state: if we follow the principles of family and kinship organization we consider necessary and proper for our society, we must ask, What kind of corrective action is needed in the law when a child is born out of wedlock? The alternative legal corrective actions can be of various kinds: punitive, educational, taking a moral stand, or remedying the "harm" to the persons involved. The alternative chosen is itself indicative of the kinship paradigm implied in the law.

In common law, illegitimate children were considered to be persons without family or kinsmen. Accordingly, they were not permitted to inherit from anyone. In states deriving their illegitimacy laws from the civil-code tradition, statutes pertaining to illegitimate children assign the ownership of those children to the mother (and to a lesser extent the acknowledged father). This proprietorship exists despite the statement found in Louisiana Civil Code Article 238 that "illegitimate children generally speaking belong to no family, and have no relations; accordingly, they are not submitted [i.e., subject] to the paternal authority, even when they have been legally acknowledged." The next article in the Louisiana Code (239) qualifies the previous article by stating

[12]   Internal Revenue Service Form W-4, Revised July 1969.

that "nevertheless nature and humanity establish certain reciprocal rights and duties between fathers and mothers and their illegitimate children." The *natural* basis for parental obligation presupposes some rights and obligations outside the law;[13] "a parent's obligations to support his child arises from the fact of paternity."[14] The priority of property rights to the mother has also been decided in the court. According to court decision, "The natural father, even when he has acknowledged the child," cannot compel the mother to part with its possession. "Moreover, care and custody of illegitimate children belong exclusively to the mother."[15]

Some states restrict proprietorship of illegitimate children to the parents themselves (particularly the mother) and permit the illegitimate child no other relatives. For example, "an illegitimate person, leaving no lawful ascendants, cannot have lawful collateral relations." A brother cannot inherit from his bastard sisters; an aunt cannot inherit from her illegitimate nephew.[16] In addition, as noted in the commentary on the early California code, "A child born illegitimately may not represent his mother or father." The only persons an illegitimate child can inherit from, according to the California code, are his descendants and his mother but not her legitimate kindred. Similarly, in the nineteenth-century laws of western territories and states, "every illegitimate child is an heir of the person who . . . acknowledges himself to be the father of such child; and in all cases is an heir of his mother; and inherits his or her estates, in whole or in part, as the case may be, in the same manner as if he had been born in lawful wedlock; but he does not represent his father or mother by inheriting any part of the estate of his or her kindred, either lineal or collateral."[17] Thus traditionally the illegitimate child has lawful descendants but not ascendants—except for his mother (and perhaps an acknowledged father), he is without a legal *genealogy.

Legitimacy of children is not derived strictly from marriage, but it has its own logic. Children can be legitimated even when

[13] David M. Schneider, *American Kinship* (Englewood Cliffs, N.J.: Prentice-Hall, Inc., 1968).

[14] Louisiana Civil Code, Article 239, Note 1.

[15] Louisiana Civil Code, Article 238, Note 4.

[16] Louisiana Civil Code, Article 238, Note 5.

[17] See statutes for Dakota Territory, 1877, Section 780; Arizona, 1865–1871, Chapter 26, Section 2; Idaho, 1863–1864, Section 316.

their parents had never been legally married to each other. For example, children of bigamous and other void marriages, children whose fathers have acknowledged them, and illegitimate children who have been adopted by an unmarried parent are all considered by law as "legitimate."

Massachusetts law (C. 207, sections 15 and 16) regards "the issue of a marriage declared void by reason of consanguinity or affinity between the parties . . . [to] be illegitimate"; yet it considers "the issue of a marriage declared void by reason of nonage, insanity or idiocy of either party . . . [to] be the legitimate issue of the parent who was capable of contracting the marriage." Many states, like Oklahoma (Ch. 4, 84–215), however, make the provision that "the issue of all marriages null in law, or dissolved by divorce, are legitimate." With regard to bigamous marriages, court decisions relating to Arkansas law (61–104) indicate that "the fact that a mother may not have been divorced from [her] former husband would not be material insofar as the legitimacy of a child is concerned." According to the Maine statutes (109–18–1003), "if the father of a child born out of wedlock adopts him or her into his family or in writing acknowledges . . . that he is the father, such child is the heir and legitimate child of his or her father." Similarly, Michigan's probate code (702.83) provides that if parents of a child born out of wedlock acknowledge "it as their child. . . . such child shall be legitimate with the identical status, rights and duties of a child born in lawful wedlock, effective from its birth."

The fact that the parents are legally married, however, does not necessarily imply the legitimacy of all their children. In the Louisiana Code (Art. 190), the husband can contest the legitimacy of a child born before the 180th day of the marriage (if he was unaware of the wife's premarital pregnancy and was not present at the registration of the birth). Moreover, the husband may disavow the child if he proves that between the 300th and the 180th day prior to the child's birth he was unable to cohabit with his wife because of a physical impossibility (e.g., distance, accidents, illness).[18] Hence, although "presumption of [the] fact of legitimacy of [a] child is one of [the] strongest known to law," even a valid marriage does not preclude illegitimacy if the father shows that the child does not "belong" to him, and he thereby disavows filiation.[19]

[18]   Louisiana Civil Code, Article 189.

[19]   See Texas statutes, 1970, Vol. 8, Supplement, p. 85.

Nor is the separation of legitimacy from marriage of the parents peculiar to the American legal system. Anthropologist Meyer Fortes points out that the mere fact of birth is insufficient for assignment of membership in a kinship unit, and "there are in all societies institutionalized procedures for the incorporation of new members into the family and the politico-jural community."[20] There are generally ritual acts of "social recognition" by which the child is accepted into the family. These rituals may include christening, the *bris* among Jews, or the ritual initiation of the son into the family cult in ancient Rome—all of which create continuity of the society through filiation, "the relationship created by the fact of being the legitimate child of one's parents."[21]

Traditionally, the legal order has been regarded as a man-made body of law superimposed on the natural order to handle (or preclude) crises, and it would thus serve the purpose of providing continuity in time, in territory, and in social relationships. If secular law is thought to be an expression of natural law, then a violation of statutory law would disturb a more basic and sacred order.[22] The act of giving birth to an illegitimate child is essentially a denial of the legal order and, consequently, of the continuity of the natural order. This violation of continuity in nature is symbolized by the rule that the illegitimate child has no legal forebearers. The illegitimate child has only "natural" rights for support and care by the mother.

With the decline of the assumption of natural law as a context for defining rights and obligations in modern society, however, an individual's right to exist as a person in the territory can no longer be relegated to some authority outside the legal order; his existence as a citizen, where all citizens are treated equally before the law, is sufficient to accord him rights of support and inheritance comparable to all other citizens. Accordingly, marriage loses its function in creating a legal basis for filiation—equality before the

---

[20] Meyer Fortes, *Kinship and the Social Order* (Chicago: Aldine Publishing Company, 1969), p. 252.

[21] Ibid., p. 253.

[22] It may be useful to distinguish between various kinds of law. Divine and natural law are related, but not identical. Divine law is handed down or revealed by God in all its applications; in some usages, natural law also has a religious origin. In other usages, however, natural law is a principle deriving from "nature," without necessarily assuming divine causation. Positive law is enacted or arbitrarily followed to cover those contingencies not embraced by divine law, and secular law refers to statutory and customary rules governing worldly rather than sacred matters.

law has already taken care of the legality of filiation. This change is reflected in American illegitimacy laws.

Early nineteenth-century American illegitimacy laws tended to ignore matters of inheritance by and from illegitimate children. For the most part they accepted the common-law conception that the illegitimate child was without ascendants and therefore had no legal status with regard to property rights. Here again the law tends to regard personal and real property as an extension of the individual. The failure of nineteenth-century law to deal explicitly with inheritance rights of illegitimate children is evident in Table 3–1.

Table 3–1 describes the intestate inheritance rights of illegitimates for forty-four states and territories as of the decade 1860–1870. Only about three fourths of the states clearly defined an illegitimate child's right to inherit from his mother (and conversely the mother's right to inherit from the child) as equal to those of a legitimate child. In about half of the states maternal kinsmen were given the right to inherit from the illegitimate child. However, most statutes and court decisions were prohibitive or generally vague with regard to inheritance rights of maternal kindred. But the vagueness in statutes and court decisions was particularly great with regard to the father's kindred. Three fourths of the statutes were silent or ambiguous with regard to the right of the father and his kin to inherit from an illegitimate child and in roughly half of the states, the rights of the illegitimate child to his father's or father's kinsmen's estates were not clearly defined. Thus, the status of the illegitimate child in nineteenth-century law was only vaguely defined in legal codes and tended to prohibit intestate inheritance from both maternal and paternal kindred.

By contrast, the twentieth century brought increased recognition of the illegitimate child as a legal person and accorded him rights which had previously been denied him. As Table 3–2 indicates, states have become more willing to permit the illegitimate child to inherit *through* the mother from her kinsmen. Whereas fewer than 20 percent of the states in 1860–1870 (eight states) permitted the illegitimate child to inherit from his mother's kindred, as of 1969 over 60 percent gave him this right. In addition, by 1969 almost all states gave the mother and her kindred the right to inherit from an illegitimate child. The status of the illegitimate child with regard to his father also improved by 1969. To be sure, many states still prohibited the child to inherit from his father or paternal kindred. Yet over half allowed the

TABLE 3-1 INHERITANCE RIGHTS OF ILLEGITIMATES WHOSE PARENTS DID NOT INTERMARRY, FOR FORTY-SEVEN STATES AND TERRITORIES, AS OF 1860–1870

Extent of Statutory or Judicial Inheritance Rights*	Maternal Side				Paternal Side			
	Child's right to inherit from:		Right to inherit from child by:		Child's right to inherit from:		Right to inherit from child by:	
	Mother	Mother's Kin	Mother	Mother's Kin	Father	Father's Kin	Father	Father's Kin
Rights of illegitimate child generally equal to those of legitimate child**	34	8	33	21	12	—	3	4
Rights of illegitimate child conditional or restricted	4	4	—	6	2	—	2	—
Statutes and court decisions vague, indefinite, or absent	4	14	10	15	19	24	36	36
Rights of inheritance prohibited	2	18	1	2	11	20	3	4

*In state statutes or accompanying notes on court decisions.
**For father, presupposes acknowledgment of illegitimate child but not marriage to mother.
Sources: See Appendix.

child to inherit grom his father, and a fourth of the states gave the child rights of inheritance through the father by representation. However, as of 1969 about half the states were still either silent or vague about the inheritance rights of the father and his kindred despite a growing tendency to accord them such rights. In balance, though, there was a general movement in inheritance laws to make the rights of an illegitimate child generally equal to those of a legitimate child.

While the trend toward removing the stigma of illegitimacy in law is generally apparent, this tendency appears to be somewhat more prevalent in states west of the Mississippi River than in eastern states. States west of the Mississippi are much more likely than those east of the Mississippi to grant the child inheritance rights from his father. The large majority of states west of the Mississippi have accorded the illegitimate child full inheritance rights in relation to his father, whereas only about a fourth east of the Mississippi have done so. This tendency suggests that the kinship paradigm prevalent in the West relies less upon the creation of marital ties in defining family status than does the kinship model found in eastern states.

As the United States entered the latter half of the twentieth century, the dramatically changing status of illegitimate children was recognized in the courts. As in the case of prohibitions on interracial marriages, few states acted until the U.S. Supreme Court handed down a landmark decision in 1968. In 1956, the Arizona Statutes (14–206) had been changed to read "every child is the legitimate child of its natural parents. . . . Every child shall inherit from its natural parents and from their kindred heir, lineal and collateral, in the same manner as children born in lawful wedlock." Yet not until 1968 did other states act. Oregon revised its statutes to read (109.060) "the legal status and legal relationships and the rights and obligations between a person and his descendants, and between a person and his parents, their descendants and kindred, are the same for all persons, whether or not the parents have been married." Similarly, North Dakota in 1969 (56–01–05) provided that "every child is hereby declared to be the legitimate child of his natural parents. . . . He shall inherit from his natural parents, and from their kindred heir, lineal and collateral."

The United States Supreme Court held in 1968, in the cases of *Levy v. Louisiana* and *Glona v. American Guarantee and Liability Insurance Company,* that a state cannot discriminate in its wrongful-death statutes solely on the basis of the legitimacy of

TABLE 3-2 INHERITANCE RIGHTS OF ILLEGITIMATES
WHOSE PARENTS DID NOT INTERMARRY,
FOR FIFTY STATES, AS OF 1969

*Extent of Statutory or Judicial Inheritance Rights**	Maternal Side				Paternal Side			
	Child's right to inherit from:		Right to inherit from child by:		Child's right to inherit from:		Right to inherit from child by:	
	Mother	*Mother's Kin*	*Mother*	*Mother's Kin*	*Father*	*Father's Kin*	*Father*	*Father's Kin*
Rights of illegitimate child generally equal to those of legitimate child**	49	32	47	44	28	13	21	15
Rights of illegitimate child conditional or restricted	1	2	—	3	1	—	1	—
Statutes and court decisions vague, indefinite, or absent	—	4	3	3	6	13	24	28
Rights of inheritance prohibited	—	12	—	—	15	24	4	7

*In state statutes or accompanying notes on court decisions.
**For father, presupposes acknowledgment of illegitimate child but not marriage to mother.

beneficiaries. These decisions have been interpreted in the broadest sense to condemn generally any classification based on legitimacy of children. Heretofore, arguments supporting discrimination against illegitimate children were founded on intentions to discourage promiscuity, to protect the family as an institution, to emphasize the relationship of the father to the family unit, and to permit the father a choice of whether or not to recognize his children. These arguments make the assumption, often found in sociological and anthropological functionalist theories, that the husband and wife (united legally in marriage) maintain a permanent household with their children. The laws presuppose a connection between legitimacy of children and the development of reciprocal relationships in the family. Like some functionalist social science theories, laws which discriminate against illegitimate children presuppose that natural law has assigned a fixed set of universal functions to the family. However, one observer, Harry D. Krause,[23] argues that in many families illegitimate children do live with their fathers but the children of divorced parents may not, and that it therefore seems unreasonable to accord the legitimate child broader rights on the basis of his living in a stable family life situation with his father and mother. Indeed, with the growing divorce rate, the correlation between legitimacy and stable family life may eventually disappear.

In effect the Supreme Court decisions of 1968 seem to have put an end to the legal construction of a "natural family" as opposed to a "family-in-law." In its decision striking down illegitimacy as a legal classification the Supreme Court viewed illegitimate persons as a minority group whose basic civil rights were being abrogated by virtue of status at birth. The perception of the court is that illegitimate persons "have no more control over their birth status than the black man has over the color of his skin. . . . Discrimination against an illegitimate child because of the marital status of his parents is in this sense clearly based on ancestry."[24]

The defense position in both the *Levy* and *Glona* cases was based on the state's power to deter illegitimacy of children by discouraging sexual intercourse among unmarried couples. The decisions separate explicitly the conception of filiation from that

---

[23] Harry D. Krause, "Equal Protection for the Illegitimate," *Michigan Law Review* 65 (1967), pp. 477–506.

[24] John C. Gray and David Rudovsky, "The Court Acknowledges the Illegitimate: *Levy v. Louisiana* and *Glona v. American Guarantee and Liability Insurance Co.*," *University of Pennsylvania Law Review* 118 (1969), p. 6.

of marriage, and they thereby reflect a general weakening of the act of marriage as a significant change in familial status. Moreover, various opinions by the Supreme Court, notably *Griswold v. Connecticut,* have condoned private sexual activities between consenting adults on the basis that the fourteenth amendment protects "certain intimate personal relationships from governmental intrusion."[25] In the light of developing concepts of individual freedom and morality, the right of the government to prohibit or discourage any immoral conduct which does no harm to the public interest is being increasingly challenged. This challenge suggests an increasing amount of experimentation possible in private, familial spheres of activity. Out of this experimentation there may evolve new conceptions of marriage which do not presuppose a stable nuclear family.

The changing views regarding illegitimacy, which have become evident in American law in the latter half of the twentieth century, seem widespread in the modern world. In 1967, a sub-commission of the Commission on Human Rights of the United Nations adopted a statement of general principles recommending equality and non-discrimination for persons born outside of wedlock. This statement of principles demands that "every person, once his filiation has been established, shall have the same legal rights as a person born in wedlock." Scandanavian countries have long established substantial equality between illegitimate and legitimate children. For example, in 1956 Norwegian law abolished all legal distinctions between them, and in 1960 Danish law provided the equal right of support and generally did not distinguish between children on the basis of legitimacy. To a lesser extent, Swedish law provides for equal support rights for illegitimate children. Other European governments are moving in the same direction. West Germany, Austria, Great Britain, and Switzerland have substantially improved rights of illegitimate children. Many Latin American countries like Bolivia, Guatemala, Panama, and Uruguay have given them equal rights. For instance, Panama's constitution says "parents have the same duties toward children born out-of-wedlock as toward those born in it. All children are equal before the law and have the same hereditary rights of intestate succession." Hence the trends observed in the United States seem to represent a worldwide movement.[26]

[25] Ibid., p. 16.

[26] Harry D. Krause, "Bastards Abroad—Foreign Approaches to Illegitimacy," *American Journal of Comparative Law* 15 (1966–1967), pp. 726–739.

The significance of the changes in laws dealing with illegitimacy is not so much that they provide the illegitimate child with a nuclear family—in effect, under the "natural"-family conception he has always had one—but more important, they give him rights and obligations in a *descent unit.* They signify the disintegration of the nuclear-family model as a "natural" entity which simultaneously embodies certain functional and legal characteristics. The shifting emphasis to descent relationships is suggested in Gray and Rudovsky's commentary regarding the use of the father's name by his illegitimate children:

> A less tangible form of discrimination which illegitimate children now suffer is the denial of a right to use their father's name. Although most illegitimates live with their mothers and might prefer to use her name, some do not and may prefer their father's name. Although the effects of this deprivation are uncertain, the disadvantage seems unjustifiable under *Levy.* It has been suggested that the denial to illegitimates of this right is reasonable because a family name serves the function of identifying an individual with a "nuclear" family group, and a father's illegitimate child will not usually be a member of this group. But identification of the "nuclear" family is probably not the purpose of names, since they are commonly shared by a much larger group of relatives, and since legitimate children, not living with their fathers, are not disqualified from using his name. If anything, a name seems to identify a group bound by certain legal relationships. Since the discriminations against illegitimates with respect to other legal relationships are now invalid under *Levy* and *Glona,* there is no longer any justification for discrimination with respect to name, assuming, of course, that paternity has been established.[27]

ADOPTION

Adoption of children is generally a stop-gap measure. It involves the transfer of the rights and obligations of persons from one family to another. In Western society adoption (a) allocates children deprived of families, (b) provides childless couples with

[27] Gray and Rudovsky, "The Court Acknowledges the Illegitimate," p. 38.

children, and (c) creates heirs to property.[28] As a way of handling crises it does not, unlike marital systems, produce stable institutions of exchange. Yet, because prohibitions of incestuous marriage may be even more stringent for persons related by adoption than for consanguineal relatives, [29] adoption must be regarded as a means for reallocating persons as family property.

Societies differ in the extent to which they use adoption to reallocate persons to kinship groups other than their natal families. Adoption tends to be more prevalent when institutions of corporate kinship or polygyny are absent. Both of these institutions are alternatives to adoption in providing care for orphaned children or transmission of property in childless marriages. In polygyny, if a wife dies, the remaining wives can care for the surviving children; if she is barren, the other wives can produce the necessary heirs. Similarly, corporate kinship groups automatically retain responsibility for orphaned children, and since property rights inhere in the corporation itself, it is not necessary for each family to produce its own heirs. For example, adoption of children tends to be rarer in African societies based on unilineal kinship corporations than in modern European countries; only as these corporate groups disappear is adoption becoming increasingly common in Africa.[30]

If adoption is a means for dealing with a crisis, the extensive use of corporate kinship groups and polygyny to deal with problems of care for orphans and of producing heirs in preliterate societies is easily understandable. In these societies, death rates are high, and life expectancy short. The probability is great that children will be bereft of parents or that married couples will outlive their heirs (or die childless). Accordingly, preliterate societies require a more stable arrangement than adoption to provide for continuity in the face of these contingencies.

Modern Western societies, however, regard mechanisms like adoption as accommodations for exceptional cases. As an auxiliary vehicle for maintaining continuity of family and kinship units in the society, adoption tends to be consistent with kinship paradigms implied in more modern provisions for continuity. The following sections will examine adoption laws to determine

---

[28] Jack Goody, "Adoption in Cross-Cultural Perspective," *Comparative Studies in Society and History* 11 (1969), pp. 55–78.

[29] Claude Lévi-Strauss, *The Elementary Structures of Kinship* (Boston: Beacon Press, 1969), p. 13.

[30] Goody, "Adoption in Cross-Cultural Perspective."

whether their historical trends reveal anything about paradigms of family and kinship prevalent in modern societies.

Comparisons of nineteenth-century adoption laws with those in effect in the latter half of the twentieth century reveal changes occurring in the conception of family membership as Western societies become highly industrialized. These comparisons include (a) cumulative memberships in families of orientation, (b) restrictions placed on rights and duties of adopter and adoptee, and (c) adoption as rebirth. American, as well as English and French law will be discussed.

Cumulative Membership in Families of Orientation

Ordinarily, adoption in American society consists of transfering legal rights and obligations over a child from one set of parents to another, and the original parents thus lose their identity as father and mother of that child. In some societies, however, the transfer does not involve extinguishing the identity of the original parents. In Truk, for example, the adopting parents accrue rights in the child only during his minority; upon adulthood he reverts back to his original kinsmen. "The adopted child acquires an additional set of kinsmen without losing the original set."[31]

In early American adoption laws, as in Truk, the transfer of the adopted child from his natural to his adoptive family was only partial. The child retained various rights and obligations in both families; these rights pertained to such matters as succession, incestuous marriage, maintenance, and obedience. For example, the Massachusetts code as of 1882 (Ch. 148, Sect. 7) stipulated that an adopted person has rights of inheritance in both his adoptive and natural families. "No person shall, by being adopted, lose his right to inherit from his natural parents or kindred." In addition, the 1882 code (Ch. 148, Sect. 6) provided that prohibitions against marriage, incest, or cohabitation of the adopted person with his natural parents and kindred would continue despite the adoption.

A review of contemporary adoption laws shows clearly the change in conception of family and kinship membership that has occurred in the twentieth century. The growing image of the family and kinship unit is one of exclusive membership in a

[31] Ward H. Goodenough, *Description and Comparison in Cultural Anthropology* (Chicago: Aldine Publishing Company, 1970), p. 31.

single family of orientation. The trend in adoption is to terminate all rights and obligations of the natural family of orientation. The Massachusetts code for 1969 (Ch. 210, Sect.7), in contrast to earlier law, provides that "A person shall by adoption lose his right to inherit from his natural parents or kindred." Similarly, the 1967 Illinois statutes (9.1–17) stipulate that "The natural parents of . . . [an adopted child] shall be relieved of all personal responsibility for such child and shall be deprived of all legal rights as respects the child, and the child shall be free from all obligations of maintenance and obedience as respects such natural parents." Other states, such as Ohio (3107.13) and Oregon (109.041) as of 1967, state expressly that the rights and obligations between the adopted child and his natural and adoptive parents exist for all legal intents and purposes "as if the adopted person had been born in lawful wedlock to his adoptive parents and had not been born to his natural parents." (Curiously, in these laws, no mention is made of incestuous-marriage prohibitions.)

Revision of adoption laws of European countries has shown a similar trend to that in the United States. In England "the general principle of the Adoption Act, 1958, is that the adopted child should rank for legal purposes as the child of its adopter and cease to be regarded as the child of its parents."[32] As in the 1926 law, adoption extinguishes "all rights, duties, obligations and liabilities" of the natural parents and assigns them to the adoptive parents. However, whereas the 1926 law reserved the adopted child's inheritance rights in his natal family, in the 1958 law, "for the purposes of the law of intestacy an adopted child ranks as the child of his adopter or adopters and not as the child of his parents, except as regards property subject to an entailed interest under a disposition made before the date of the [adoption] order."[33]

France has introduced two kinds of adoption to supplement the old partial adoption of adults under the Code Napoleon. In 1939, the Civil Code (Sections 368—370) introduced the procedure of adoptive legitimation, whereby the child leaves his natural family completely and enters that of his adopters. In adoptive legitimation, ordinarily the adoptive parents and their relatives acquire the same rights and obligations as if the adopted child had been born within the marriage while the natural family, on the other hand, loses all rights of succession. Adoptive

---

[32]   E. L. Johnson, *Family Law* (London: Sweet and Maxwell, 1965), p. 293.

[33]   W. Clarke Hall and Justin Clarke Hall, *The Law of Adoption and Guardianship of Infants* (London: Butterworth, 1928), p. 33 and Johnson, *Family Law*, p. 294.

legitimation, however, was permissible only for children under seven years of age whose parents were unknown, dead, or had abandoned them. To cover other situations in which adoption was warranted, procedures for "full" adoption were created in the Civil Code (Sections 343–367) after 1958. This kind of adoption breaks the adopted child's ties with his original family with the consent of the natural parents (C.C.354).[34]

The trend indicated in the adoption laws of England and France is also apparent in other European countries. In the Soviet Union, for example, "adoption severs all legal ties with the natural parents, in order to protect the child from intrusion on his adoptive relationship. Once adoption is completed, the child is referred to as if he were born in wedlock to his adoptive parents."[35]

In summary, this survey of revisions of adoption laws in the twentieth century suggests that a change has occurred in the conception of the nature of family and kinship organization in Europe as well as the United States. The nineteenth-century conception was that membership in families of orientation was cumulative. In addition to his natural family of orientation, an individual could join another family of orientation "artificially" by law, through adoption. Because of this cumulative aspect, membership in families of orientation could be regarded as permanent. The twentieth-century laws, however, emphasize the exclusive character of membership in a family of orientation. Adoption then cannot simply add one set of relationships to another but must replace one family with another. Even ties to the family of orientation cannot be considered as permanent. Changes in laws of adoption are consistent with those pertaining to incestuous marriage prohibitions in that both kinds of laws imply a trend away from cumulative membership of individuals in more than one family of orientation.

Restrictions on Adoptive Relationships

The assumption in nineteenth-century law, that an individual could have membership in two families of orientation simul-

---

[34]   P. H. Lawson, A. E. Anton, and L. Neville Brown, *Amos and Walton's Introduction to French Law* (London: Oxford University Press, 1967), pp. 78–79, 299, 303.

[35]   Bernice Q. Madison, *Social Welfare in the Soviet Union* (Stanford, Calif.: Stanford University Press, 1968), p. 157.

taneously, required that rights and duties of the adopted person in each family be explicated to avoid conflict. This requirement led to a strict legal interpretation of obligations defined by law, and it restricted the kinds of relationships created through adoption.[36] Ordinarily, obligations for custody and care of the child were assigned to the adoptive parents, while the child's rights of succession in his adoptive family were limited. Nonconflicting constraints, such as prohibitions of incestuous marriage, sometimes extended to both natural and adoptive parents.

One restriction on the adoptive relationship prevalent in nineteenth-century law was that rights and obligations created by adoption did not extend to other members of the adoptive parent's family of orientation. Massachusetts law in 1882 (Ch. 148, Sect. 7) provides "as to succession to property, a person adopted shall take the same share of property . . . that he would have taken if born to such [adopting] parent in lawful wedlock, and he shall stand in regard to the legal descendants, but to no other of the kindred of such parent, in the same position as if so born to him." However, amendments in 1965 and 1967 revised this statute so that now the adopted person "shall stand to the kindred of such adopting parent in the same position as if so born to him." Provisions in other contemporary codes are similar. Oregon law (1967, 109.050), for example, states that "an adopted child bears the same relation to his adoptive parents and their kindred in every respect pertaining to the relation of parent and child as he would if he were the natural child of such parent."

However, some states, like Tennessee, are still guided in their adoption laws by the conception of cumulative membership in families of orientation. Consistent with this conception, Tennessee laws pertaining to incestuous marriage still adhere to Biblical prohibitions against marrying in-laws. The discussion of court decisions in the Tennessee 1955 statutes (36–101, Decision #3) describes the basis for restricting adoptive relationship as follows:

> Statutes relating to adoption of children, being in derogation of the common law, are strictly construed, and will not be held, in the absence of express provisions to that effect, to intend to confer rights to custody of children upon persons who are not parties to the record of adoption, and who have

[36] George P. Proctor, "Parent and Child—Adoption—Effect on Natural Parent's Duty to Support," *Illinois Bar Journal* 26 (1938), pp. 211–213.

not assumed any of the legal obligations of an adoptive parent.

Accordingly, since Tennessee law does not regard adoption as "a natural right" (36–101, Decision #4), "an adopted child does not inherit from the collateral relatives of its adoptive parent" (36–126, Decision #7).

Similar restrictions on the adoptive relationship appeared in English and French law prior to the mid-twentieth century. The 1926 English law followed a strict interpretation. It stipulated that "An adoption order shall not . . . [automatically] confer on the adopted child any right to or interest in property as a child of the adopter." Likewise, the old French Civil Code restricted the rights of the adopted person. Section 350 of the Code stated, "The adopted shall not acquire any rights of succession to property of the relatives of the adopter"; his only link was with the adopter.

The changes in the English and French laws revised the family status of adopted persons. In England, with regard to the law of intestacy, "a child adopted jointly by two spouses ranks as a brother or sister of the whole blood of a child . . . of both spouses." However, with regard to prohibited degrees of consanguinity, the adopted child remains an outsider; he can marry a natural child of his adopting parent.[37] In France, under adoptive legitimation, formal acknowledgment by the parents of the adopters gives the adopted child full rights of succession from them.

Retention of restrictions on the relationship between the person adopted and his adoptive family is not limited to Western Europe. Despite sharp differences from England and France in laws of inheritance, the Soviet Union has similar legal restrictions on the adoption relationship. Although "adopted children and their descendants have the same personal and property rights and duties to the adopter as do the adopter's natural children . . . this legal tie applies only to the adopted child and the adopter: it does not extend to the relationships between the adopted child and members of the adopter's family." However, some Soviet authorities regard this restriction as a survival of the old regime.

Criticizing this feature of the law, one Soviet scholar states that it is justifiable "only when the determining role in adoption is played by property interests, interests of inher-

---

[37] Johnson, *Family Law*, p. 294.

itance, when broad rights of the adopted child in the family of the adopter can bring about material loss to the heirs"—in short, in a capitalist state and not in a socialist one.[38]

Generally, legal modifications of rights and obligations of adopted persons follow the trend both of exclusiveness of membership in families of orientation and of providing the adoptee with a new kindred. In both the United States and Western Europe, the adoption laws have shown this shift regardless of the rationale for adoption, of definitions of persons capable of adopting or being adopted, or of procedure in the nineteenth century (or early twentieth century). At the same time the revisions suggest that the changes in kinship paradigms implied in legal codes have been only partial and do not represent a complete displacement of one conceptual model by another. The European countries in particular indicate a reluctance to depart from traditional norms and conceptions regardless of changes in their political and economic structures.

Adoption as Rebirth

Where adoption implies a full transfer of the child from his natural to adoptive family, efforts are ordinarily made to provide him with a new legal identity. Symbolic of this new identity is a change in name and the issuance of a new birth certificate. Usually, the reasons given for preparing another birth certificate are (a) avoiding the possible stigma attached to adoption, (b) leaving to the adoptive parents the prerogative of telling the child whether or not he has been adopted, and/or (c) precluding the tracing of the natural parentage. Regardless of the reason, the conception that membership in families of orientation is not cumulative suggests that a change of membership itself demands a loss of the old kinship identity and the gaining of a new identity. Hence the act of adoption is an act of rebirth of a new legal person.

Modern American law characterizes this rebirth in ways exemplified by the Ohio statutes (1967, 3705.18), which state:

> . . . The department shall issue a new birth certificate using the child's adopted name and the names of and data concerning the adoptive parents and such new birth certificate shall

---

[38] Madison, *Social Welfare*, p. 157.

have the same overall appearance as certificate which would
have been issued . . . if the adopted child had been born to
the adoptive parents. . . . Upon the issuance of such new
certificate of birth, the original certificate of birth shall cease
to be a public record.

The 1926 English law also provided for the reissuance of a
new birth certificate, but it required that this certificate indicate
that the child had been adopted. The birth record of the child
prior to the adoption, however, was closed to public inspection.[39]
The Births and Deaths Registration Act, 1953, s.33, went even
further by authorizing the issuance of birth certificates without
any mention of adoption.[40]

The issuance of new birth certificates and the removal of old
birth information from public records implies a stigma attached to
adoption. The adopted child's previous family history, for all
practical purposes, is completely erased as if his natural family
had never existed.[41] This action in deleting the past history of the
adopted child, while it is performed presumably for the child's
benefit, has the consequence of reinforcing the conception of
exclusive membership in a single family of orientation as the
individual's primary kinship identity.

DISCUSSION: TRENDS IN SUPPORT, LEGITIMACY, AND ADOPTION LAWS

The trends in laws pertaining to support, legitimacy, and
adoption suggest that profound changes have occurred in the
conception of family and kinship during the past century in the
United States. They indicate a decline in the potency of the
"natural"-family paradigm as a guiding principle in family law.

The kinship paradigm implied in legal codes in the nineteenth century permitted membership in more than one family of
orientation. Historically, membership in two families of orientation was made possible by being born into one family and married
or adopted into another. The family of birth was a "natural"
family of orientation and the family which the individual joined

---

[39] Hall and Hall, *Law of Adoption*, pp. 44–48.

[40] Johnson, *Family Law*, p. 296.

[41] Compare this "defamilization" with the process of being "depersoned" in Orwell's *1984*.

by virtue of marriage or adoption became an "artificial" relationship, created by law. Since the family of birth was "natural," rights and obligations in that family were ordinarily governed by religious or natural law. The natural tie was considered more basic than the artificial bonds. The law defined the man-made relationship. Family relationships in law were supposed to express the natural relationships, and marriage and adoption gave an individual rights in his family or orientation by law comparable to those in his natural family. From the perspective of intimate-kin groups, the husband and wife were symbolically incorporated into each other's family of orientation while retaining their old status in their own natural family. Consequently, the two families of orientation shared the membership of the married children. Such an arrangement would create a tightly interwoven network of related families. Folk and religious traditions could be sustained in the name of the joint interests of the two families of orientation allied by marriage or adoption.

When membership is restricted to only one family of orientation, the distinction between natural and artificial families becomes meaningless. Whereas under the natural-law conception of kinship, an individual has "natural" rights as opposed to the civil rights gained through law, this distinction becomes useless in the legal-family paradigm. Only that family of orientation which is chartered by the law is recognized as valid; the state has become the exclusive licensing agency in ascribing membership in families of orientation. Under this paradigm, the family becomes merely a subsection of the state, drawing its license to exist from state authorities.

If family rights and obligations are defined as subsets of general civil rights and obligations, there is no apparent justification for making a sharp distinction between nuclear family as a natural entity and the more extensive kindred. The movement evident in revisions of illegitimacy and adoption laws (and less clearly observable in support laws) over the past century is toward endowing indigent, illegitimate, and adopted persons with rights not only in nuclear families but also in entire kindreds. Under common law, an individual was obligated to support only his family of procreation; early in English and American legal history this obligation was extended to cover indigent parents, and many states have expanded this duty to include needy siblings and grandparents as well. Nineteenth-century illegitimacy laws, meant to protect the integrity of the nuclear family, vested the bastard child with some rights of inheritance from its mother and, in a few states, from its father; in general the laws placed strong restrictions upon inheritance by representation, thereby depriving the child of benefits derived from having a kindred. In the twentieth century, by statute and by Supreme Court decision, illegitimate children have gained both familial and kinship rights comparable to those of legitimate children. The trend in adoption laws is similar. Legal modifications, which have given adoptive families exclusive rights in the child, have also extended the adopted child's rights in relation to his adoptive parents' kindreds. These changes in support, illegitimacy, and adoption laws indicate a shift away from emphasis on nuclear-family bonds to an accent on more extensive kinship ties in defining rights and obligations.

The increased stress on kinship ties in support, illegitimacy, and adoption laws has significant implications for family organization. The earlier emphasis on the integrity of the nuclear family presupposes a strong and permanent marital bond between husband and wife. The decline of this emphasis and the increasing importance of the kindred, however, suggests that a greater weight is now being given to descent ties in laws governing family organization. In terms of kinship paradigms, the findings indicate that the trend is away from the Biblical kinship model and its reliance on firm marital ties and toward a sharpening of rights and obligations associated with the legal-family model and its dependence on ties of descent and filiation.

4

Family and Estate

Ever since Henry Maine wrote *Ancient Law* in 1861 social scientists have sought to connect characteristics of society—and especially kinship organization—with patterns of succession of property rights. Chapter 1 suggested that in highly industrialized societies, people can best insure the welfare of their kindred by investing time, energy, and wealth in individual relatives. This investment implies only a small role of affines in maintaining the stability of marriage and much emphasis upon the enhancement of the worth of family members related by blood. Since any family member is potentially successful, the transmission of wealth from one generation to the next should maximize opportunities for all descendants. Hence, in highly industrialized societies, intestacy should partition estates among consanguineal kin rather than devolve them entirely upon a single heir.

In peasant societies, partible inheritance (that is, dividing estates among heirs) is associated with the availability of land.[1] Where land is scarce, estates are generally transmitted intact to a single heir from one generation to the next. In the past, the scarcity of land has permitted the development of strong and independent classes of nobility through their ability to retain control over large territories. It was only in countries with highly

[1] Walter Goldschmidt and Evalyn Jacobson Kunkel, "The Structure of the Peasant Family," *American Anthropologist* 73 (1971), pp. 1058–1076.

centralized bureaucracies (such as traditional China, Russia, and India) that the power of landholding families could be restricted through partible inheritance.

In England's commercial development, the scarcity of land, capital and unbound labor seems to have required a single-heir system to accumulate land and capital power to develop a mobile labor force. In America during the eighteenth century, however, land was abundant, and immigration provided mobile workers. The American colonists found English inheritance practices inconsistent with their own needs. Opposition to *primogeniture and entail of landed estates came both in New England and in Virginia, where English laws governing succession of property were in effect.[2] Some New Englanders with close ties to English nobility did practice entail; but in general landed estates in New England changed hands frequently. Many Virginians tried to circumvent English inheritance laws. In the decade preceding the American Revolution, roughly one sixth of all acts passed in the Virginia legislature dealt with docking entail provisions for specific estates.[3] Because of heavy investment in tobacco in Virginia, old lands were continually wearing out, and families moved to new ones. Since entail is designed for fixed estates, not varying ones, the Virginia land owners found perpetual entail of land a nuisance. In New England as well, the abundance of cheap land made entail and primogeniture superfluous.[4] Thus, it is reasonable that in America, intestacy laws have always prescribed partible inheritance.

What are the different social consequences of partible and impartible inheritance? According to some observers, the rise of industrialization in England can be attributed, in part, to primogeniture. Habakkuk notes, "It is significant that England, the country of earliest factories and regions of industrial concentration, was the country where, with a few minor exceptions, younger children had no claim at common law to any share of their father's estate."[5] He then suggests that the rapid development of German industry was facilitated by a comparable pattern

[2] Richard B. Morris, *Studies in the History of American Law* (New York: Columbia University Press, 1930) pp. 86–92.

[3] Clarence R. Keim, "Influence of Primogeniture and Entail in the Development of Virginia," Ph.D. dissertation, University of Chicago, 1926, p. 136.

[4] Ibid., pp. 138–154.

[5] H. J. Habakkuk, "Family Structure and Economic Change in Nineteenth-Century Europe," *Journal of Economic History* 15 (1955), pp. 1–12.

of inheritance, while partible inheritance, characteristic of the Russian *mir* and the French system of succession under the Napoleonic Civil Code, inhibited industrialization.

Habakkuk proposes that single-heir inheritance has had a direct influence on industrialization because systems like primogeniture produce: (a) an increased concentration of capital in the family line of single heirs instead of depleting this capital among heirs, (b) a highly mobile labor market consisting of non-heirs, since they have no continuing interest in their family's enterprises, and (c) an increase in population by non-heirs, who become part of the industrial labor force, and who marry early and in increased numbers.

Insofar as a system of inheritance has important consequences for social structure, an examination of laws of succession and inheritance may shed light on the characteristics of natural-family and legal-family paradigms. The natural-family view of marriage as the joining of husband and wife into "one flesh" is one which affects numerous rules of family life; it is the basis of (a) extending marital and sexual prohibitions to the spouse's family of orientation, (b) for regarding membership in the spouse's family as permanent, and (c) for emphasizing the crucial significance of the marital bond in maintaining the nuclear family as a fundamental unit. The concept that husband and wife are of one flesh is also the basis for viewing marriage as a means for consolidating kin group property: marriage then fuses the couple's families of orientation by the creation of a new nuclear family. These families had been previously unrelated or at least more distantly related. The whole system of family and kinship organization, including mode of inheritance, is then aimed at consolidating resources of families fused by marriage. In this manner, more powerful and wealthier families can maintain or improve their political, economic, or social position.

The conception of marriage as a fusion of previously unrelated families suggests that even where partible inheritance is practiced, certain kinds of inheritance rules will predominate. Any nuclear family represents an actual *fusion* of parental nuclear families, which themselves represent a fusion of other parental families, and so on *ad infinitum.* The precise relationship of any heir to a decedent would be less important than his distance from the decedent's nuclear family. Hence, laws governing intestacy according to the natural-family model should emphasize kinship distance from the decedent and should give little attention to the precise lines of descent or to heirs' specific generations.

In contrast to inheritance rules aimed at consolidating resources of previously unrelated families, those laws deriving from
the legal-family paradigm emphasize descent ties rather than
nuclear-family relationships. Insofar as the legal-family model
does not presuppose permanent marital bonds, it would be
unreasonable to utilize marriage as a means for consolidating
family resources. Instead, inheritance laws provide a vehicle for
maintaining the welfare of persons of closely related lines of
descent. Since lines of descent tend to proliferate as the population increases with each generation, inheritance laws (particularly
those in intestacy cases) must be constructed to minimize the
dispersion of family property over a series of generations.[6]

The kinds of rules covered by intestacy laws under the
legal-family paradigm differ from those of the natural-family
model. Since descent ties are stressed in the legal-family model,
the nature of consanguineal relationships must be taken into
account in devolving estates. For example, paternal and maternal
lines of descent and heir's generation may become significant
factors in partitioning estates. How these affect legal statuses will
be indicated later.

This chapter, relying mainly on American law, will discuss
trends in intestacy laws from the perspective of the natural-family
and legal-family paradigms. It will suggest how the shift to the
legal-family model represents a departure from the function of the
family to maintain the traditional system of social stratification in
the society, a system based on consolidating nuclear-family
resources. It will focus in large measure upon the content of
intestacy laws in the United States, particulary on the priorities of
distribution when the decedent has left no descendants. To
indicate consistency in sets of law, it will examine the relationship between intestacy provisions and law pertaining to incestuous marriage. Later in the chapter, the analysis of priorities in
the distribution of estates will cover nineteenth as well as
twentieth-century law. The historical study will indicate trends
with regard to sex differentiation and lineal emphasis.

The review here concerns intestacy, and American testate
rules of succession, it should be noted, are more flexible than
European practices. Under the French Civil Code, for example,

---

[6] However, inasmuch as the legal-family model defines the family as a sub-unit of the state,
many of the resources which might otherwise be handled and transmitted in the family are
held and administered by the state. It is then no longer necessary to make a sharp distinction
between family and state as proprietors of resources. Inheritance under the legal-family model
may be regarded as an adjunct to the allocation of the state's resources.

testamentary inheritance is limited in that a person cannot deprive his children of their legal share without formally disinheriting them; the amount set aside depends upon the number of children. In contrast, "ours is one of the few legal systems in the world which does not impose some degree of restraint upon the power of a *testator to disinherit his lineal descendants."[7]

INTESTACY LAWS

In every society with statutory codes, laws exist which regulate the transmission of property of a decedent to his heirs. Although modern industrial societies permit testators to choose heirs, many people die without making a *will. Laws governing the succession of property pertain for the most part to the inheritance rights of kinsmen of a person dying intestate (without leaving a will).

Laws regulating intestacy are intended to reflect what might have happened had the deceased person left a will. In effect, these laws are supposed to represent the norms of succession which actually are operative in the society at any particular time. Table 4–1 presents the distribution of estates by genealogical relationship of the survivors by testacy in Michigan.[8] In the comparison of the devolution of estates for persons dying with and without wills, there is a general similarity in the proportions of heirs falling into each genealogical category. Findings of a Wisconsin study are similar.[9] In his analysis of wills in Cook County, Illinois, Dunham found that deviations from intestacy laws were generally made in "unusual circumstances."[10] As in the Wisconsin study, the major deviation in Illinois was the allotment of a larger share to the surviving spouse than provided in intestacy laws.[11] Like the other investigations, a study in Cleveland, Ohio by Sussman, Cates, and Smith found that normally a testate individual wills

---

[7]   Olin L. Browder, Jr., "Recent Patterns of Testate Succession in the United States and England," *Michigan Law Review* 67 (1969), p. 1307.

[8]   Ibid., p. 1306.

[9]   Edward H. Ward and J. H. Beuscher, "The Inheritance Process in Wisconsin," *Wisconsin Law Review* 1950 volume, pp. 393–426.

[10]   Allison Dunham, "The Method, Process and Frequency of Wealth Transmission at Death," *University of Chicago Law Review* 30 (1963), p. 252.

[11]   Ward and Beuscher, "The Inheritance Process in Wisconsin," p. 413.

TABLE 4-1 DISTRIBUTION OF ESTATES BY GENEALOGICAL RELATIONSHIPS OF SURVIVORS TO DECEDENTS AND BY TESTACY (WASHTENAW COUNTY, MICHIGAN, 1963)

Genealogical Relationship of Survivors	Percent of Testate Estates	Percent of Intestate Estates
Spouse and Issue	29	29
Issue	36	33
Collaterals	25	23
Spouse and Collaterals	6	5
Spouse	1	1
Spouse and a Parent	—	—*
Father or Mother	—*	6
No Heirs	3	2
Total N	(187)	(159)

*Less than one percent.
Table based on Olin L. Browder, Jr., "Recent Patterns of Testate Succession in the United States and England," *Michigan Law Review*, 67 (1969), Table 1, p. 1306.

his estate to his spouse even when there are children living; ultimately the estate will devolve to the children anyway.[12] In most cases, departures from the intestate rules of distribution are made on the basis of need, appreciation for assistance or service, or estrangement, that is, circumstances which cannot be handled by statute. "Once the basic decision to be testate has been made, the location of the testator on the kin network is the most important factor in the pattern of distribution chosen by him."[13] Thus at least for the midwestern states analyzed, the intestacy laws seem to represent generally the norms of succession prevalent in the society.[14]

The fact that succession is a phenomenon associated with kinship places at least two constraints on intestacy laws. First, restrictions are influenced by the nature of genealogy in that the genealogical relationships define the different kinds of relatives to whom the decedent has ties. Second, the codes must take into account the contingencies of birth, age, death, and marriage,

[12] Marvin B. Sussman, Judith N. Cates, and David T. Smith, *The Family and Inheritance* (New York: Russell Sage Foundation, 1970).

[13] Ibid., p. 120.

[14] Browder, "Recent Patterns of Testate Succession," p. 306.

which give the genealogical map of each family a distinct character. Hence, the intestacy codes must first establish a rank order of priority of succession by persons in the various parts of the genealogy and, second, they must allow for contingencies which arise through the acquisition or loss of kin who normally succeed the decedent.

In modern industrial societies, the primary heirs of a person dying intestate are his children. A review of legal codes reveals that there is little variation in awarding estates to children. Without exception, if a child without descendants precedes his parents in death, his share is apportioned to his brothers and sisters; if he leaves descendants, his share is distributed to his own children by representation (or per *stirpes). Generally, the decedent's spouse is also included as an heir, but sometimes the spouse is awarded property by virtue of falling into a special legal category (such as the recipient of a lifetime *dower). In this manner, provisions are made for maintaining the spouse, but without the implications of descent inherent in the concepts of succession and heirship.

Most interesting are the provisions made when a decedent leaves no descendants. In providing for this contingency, the intestacy laws reveal a variety of kinship assumptions when assigning the right of succession to others in the decedent's genealogy. In the absence of descendants, should the entire estate go to the spouse, to the parents, or to the siblings? What should the ranking of priority be among these? And if there are no spouses, parents, or siblings, should the estate be divided equally between paternal and maternal relatives? If so, between which ones?

From the perspective of kinship, the assigning of priorities of succession involves choosing which dimensions of genealogy are more fundamental than others in kinship organization: generation, genealogical proximity, lineality, sex, consanguinity, and so on. Each set of priorities in determining succession implies different assumptions regarding the rules of kinship organization.

The following section examines recent statutes regarding succession in the fifty states with respect to priorities in inheritance. These priorities are interpreted in light of their implications for characterizing the natural- and legal-family models. In most instances, the 1969 codes provide the basis of analysis. The analysis concerns: (a) the partitioning of estates among spouse, parents, and siblings when the decedent left no descendants, (b) the distribution of estates in the absence of spouse, children, parents, and siblings, and (c) the relationship between laws of succession and those governing incestuous marriage. A later section of this chapter reviews early statutes to show trends in inheritance law which took place as the legal-family paradigm emerged to become an organizing principle.

SPOUSE, FAMILY, AND KINSMAN

Spouse and Family of Orientation

The legal priorities for assigning estates to the spouse and family of orientation of a decedent are related to the role of marriage in modern family and kinship organization. Is the spouse to be placed on an equal footing with the decedent's parents or with siblings? Should the spouse be given priority over anyone in the decedent's family of orientation, or should everyone be placed in the same category and share the estate equally? Each of these alternatives carries with it a different connotation for the relationships between a person and his spouse and his family of orientation.

If, in the order of priorities, the spouse *shares* the estate (either perpetually or for *life) with the parents of the decedent—but with siblings only when the parents are dead—this situation may be interpreted as follows: by being placed in the same category of succession as the parents, the spouse may be regarded as a member of the same family unit; the law symbolizes, as an expression of the natural-family model, his incorporation into the decedent's family of orientation. Eventually, the portion of the estate assigned to the parents (if they are not already dead) will be distributed among the decedent's brothers and sisters and their descendants. Except where the spouse receives a life estate, this form of succession splits the estate so that both the decedent's and his spouse's families of orientation will ultimately share the property.

If the ranking of priorities assigns the *entire* estate to the spouse—and the parents and siblings inherit only when there is no spouse—the following interpretation is offered: the spouse is in a category of succession separate from the decedent's family of orientation. This mode of succession implies a sharp differentiation between consanguineous and affinal kinsmen. In effect, by placing the spouse in a separate inheritance category, this form of succession suggests the presence of a loose marital alliance now broken by death; it is possible to regard the transfer of the entire estate to the surviving spouse as compensating the widow (or widower) and her kin for the loss sustained. Ultimately, the surviving spouse's family will be the recipients of the estate in its entirety.

After a discussion in the next section on procedures for computing degrees of relationship, data regarding the relative priorities of spouse and parents in intestacy laws will be analyzed. But a discussion of these procedures is necessary to set the stage for a comparison between priorities given to the spouse and distribution outside the immediate family. The analysis is intended to indicate how classifying the spouse with the decedent's parents expresses the natural-family model, whereas treating the spouse separately derives from the legal-family model.

Dimensions of Succession
Outside the Immediate Family

When neither spouse nor any member of the decedent's family of orientation is alive (and there are no direct descendants), how is the estate partitioned? In American legal codes, there are two general patterns: one pattern is an equal division of the estate between paternal and maternal relatives; the other is a distribution of the estate among persons in the nearest degree of kinship regardless of the nature of the relationship.

Legal provision for the division of the estate into two equal parts—half going to the paternal kin and the other half to the maternal kin—is found in only thirteen states. In most statutes, the term *moiety* is used to describe the estate halves assigned to maternal and paternal kin. The emphasis on lines of descent suggests that the moiety system is related to the legal-family model.

The remainder of the states, however, provide for distribution of estates outside the immediate family by the nearest degree of kinship. Based on *cognatic relationships (that is, tracing descent of individuals to their common ancestors) the procedure followed in American law emphasizes the extent of filiation existing among kinsmen.[15] The closer the cognatic ties, presumably the stronger are the obligations and sentiments normally associated with kinship. Following the Roman procedure, degree of kinship is

[15] Meyer Fortes, *Kinship and the Social Order* (Chicago: Aldine Publishing Company, 1969), pp. 267–269.

computed in American civil law in a manner best illustrated by
Louisiana statutes, which had been derived from the French Civil
Code:

Art. 889. Degrees of relationship

Art. 889. The propinquity of consanguinity is established by the number of generations, and each generation is
called a degree.

Art. 890. Direct and collateral consanguinity

Art. 890. The series of degrees form the line; the series
of degrees between persons who descend from one another is
called direct or lineal consanguinity, and the series of degrees
between persons who do not descend from one another, but
spring from a common ancestor, is called the collateral line or
collateral consanguinity.

The direct line is divided into a direct line descending
and a direct line ascending. The first is that which connects
the ancestor with those who descend from him; the second is
that which connects a person with those from whom he
descends.

Art. 891. Direct line, degrees of relationship

Art. 891. In the direct line there are as many degrees as
there are generations. Thus the son is with regard to the
father, in the first degree, the grandson in the second, and *vice
versa* with regard to the father and grandfather towards the
sons and grandsons.

Art. 892. Collateral line, degrees of relationship

Art. 892. In the collateral line the degrees are counted
by the generations from one of the relations up to the common
ancestor exclusively, and from the common ancestor to the
other relations.

Thus brothers are related in the second degree, uncle and
nephew in the third degree; cousins german in the fourth, and
so on.

In contrast to the civil code used in almost all American
inheritance laws, computation of degrees of kinship under canon
law—which was later applied in English common law (and
currently in Georgia law)—determines the degree of kinship by
the number of generations from the nearest common ancestor to
the intestate and to the claimant. In the canon law procedure for
counting degrees of relationship, there are as many degrees
between two kinsmen as there are generations (or ascendants)
from them to a common ancestor. If the two lines of descent from a

common ancestor are unequal, the line which includes more generations determines the degree of relationship between them. (The common ancestor is not counted in computing degrees of relationship by this technique.) According to the canon law procedure, the following are all third-degree relatives of EGO (i.e., the person of reference): (a) his second cousins, (b) his first cousins-once-removed, (c) his great-aunts and great-uncles, and (d) his great-grandparents.[16] The differences between the civil law and canon law methods for counting degrees of relationships are illustrated for these relatives in Figure 1. In canon law, one counts *down* from the common ancestor to the two relatives whose genealogical distance is to be ascertained, taking the longer of the two lines (when they are unequal) as the degree of relationship. In civil law, one starts with EGO and then traces the ascending and descending relatives through whom genealogical ties are made, with each relative adding one degree of relationship. According to civil law procedure, (a) second cousins are sixth-degree relatives, (b) first cousins-once-removed are fifth-degree relatives, (c) great-aunts and great-uncles fourth degree, and (d) great-grandparents third degree. To repeat, almost invariably American statutes apply the civil law procedure to calculate degrees of relationships; Georgia alone follows the canon law method.

Some states which use nearest degree of kinship (or "next of kin") to determine distribution outside the immediate family impose a second criterion: when two potential heirs are of equal degree of kinship to a decedent as collateral kin, the common ancestor for the decedent and these potential heirs is taken into account. If the collateral kin are related to the decedent through different common ancestors, the one whose ancestor was closer in degree of relationship to the decedent is given preference in the distribution of the estate. Thus, suppose that a man dies intestate and leaves a first-cousin and a great-uncle, both of whom are fourth-degree relatives according to civil law procedures for calculating genealogical distance. In this case, the cousin would be given priority in the estate over the great-uncle although both are equidistant genealogically from the decedent. The basis for the cousin's priority is that his common ancestor is the decedent's grandfather, whereas the common ancestor for the great-uncle is the decedent's great-grandfather. The criterion of the closest ancestor provides a mechanism for assigning priority to persons of later generations and adheres to the purpose of succession as

[16] H. A. Ayrinhac, *Marriage Legislation in the New Code of Canon Law*, rev. P. J. Lydon, (New York: Benziger Brothers, 1946), p. 168.

FIGURE 1 COMPUTATION OF DEGREES OF RELATIONSHIP, BY CIVIL LAW AND CANON LAW METHODS

Civil Law Method: Count from EGO to other relative.

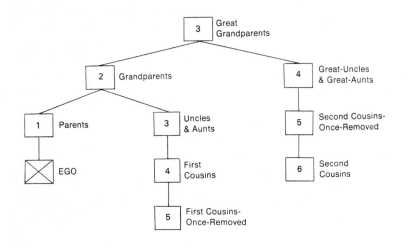

Canon Law Method: Count from common ancestor ⊠ both to EGO and to other relative, with the larger number as the degree of relationship.

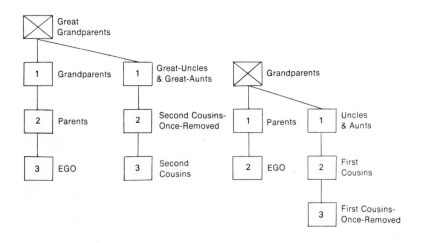

being the transmission of property to descending generations. The criterion of preference for kinsmen related through the closest ancestor therefore emphasizes classification of kinship by lineal descent rather than merely closeness of kinship ties. However, this criterion seems weaker than the concept of paternal and maternal moieties as an indicator of the lineal descent principle.

The following sections analyze data based on state legal codes regarding the transmission of property when someone dies intestate without leaving any direct descendants. First, the discussion deals with the relationship between rank order of succession within and outside the immediate family. Second, it is concerned with the association between distribution outside the immediate family and prohibitions relating to incestuous marriage. Third, for those states in which succession outside the immediate family is to nearest degree of kin without regard to maternal or paternal connection, the relationship between preference for kin related through nearest common ancestor and incestuous-marriage prohibitions are examined. These analyses are intended to indicate further how natural- and legal-family paradigms operate as organizing principles in law.

Succession Within and
Outside Immediate Family

The earlier discussion of statutes pertaining to succession suggested that treating the spouse together with the parents implies a conception of family and kinship different from that where the spouse is placed in a separate category. In the former case, consistent with the natural-family model, the spouse is symbolically fused with the decedent's family of orientation, whereas in the latter case, following the legal-family model, the spouse is treated separately from the decedent's family and presumably remains identified with his own natal family and kinship unit.

If there is a basic organizing principle operating here, the treatment of the spouse in inheritance laws should be related to distribution outside the nuclear family: (a) If the spouse retains his primary identity with his own family of orientation, so should each of his parents, and so on. As a result of this progression, maternal and paternal kin should be categorized separately, and property should accordingly pass to maternal and paternal kin separately, with each kinship unit retaining its independent rights in its members. Hence, the treatment of the spouse in a category apart from the decedent's parents should be associated empirically with the division of the estate into moieties—half going to maternal and the other half to paternal kin. (b) Where fusion of the spouse with the family of orientation occurs, however, the differentiation between maternal and paternal kin is unnecessary, and the nearest degree of kinship regardless of the specific relationship should be important in setting priorities for succession of estates.

Table 4–2 presents data on current intestacy laws of the fifty states. It is necessary to make several decisions somewhat arbitrarily in classifying states in the table. First, in order to avoid contradictory rights regarding the surviving spouse, where intestacy laws governing personal property and real estate still differ, the data are based on personal-property inheritance. Second, in some states, when there are no children, the spouse is awarded an initial amount (varying from $3000 in Michigan to $100,000 in South Dakota) and then shares the remainder evenly with the decedent's parents; these states are classified as placing the spouse only partially in a separate category from the parents. Third, limits placed on the genealogical distance of kinsmen who can inherit as next of kin are ignored. (For example, Missouri limits inheritance to ninth degree of kin, Kansas to sixth-degree kin, and Maryland to tenth-degree kin; New Mexico limits affinity to the eighth degree.) Fourth, community-property states (such as California and Nevada) are classified according to rules covering *community property rather than the separate property of husband and wife.

Table 4–2 shows the order of succession within the immediate family as compared with the mode of inheritance in the larger kindred when spouse and all members of the decedent's family of orientation are dead. As earlier, the priorities are those where the intestate has left no descendants. One third of the states in which the spouse succeeds to the full estate use the concept of moieties when estates are distributed outside the nuclear family; in contrast, just one state requiring the spouse to share the estate with parents utilizes moieties in distributing estates outside the immediate family. Hence, the lineal emphasis of paternal and maternal moieties is related to treating the spouse separately from the intestate's parents.

As for the nearest-ancestor criterion, however, the data are inconclusive. About the same proportion of next-of-kin states and nearest-ancestor states require the spouse to share the estate with

---

TABLE 4–2 ORDER OF INHERITANCE WITH REGARD TO SPOUSE
AND IMMEDIATE FAMILY (WHEN THERE ARE NO ISSUE)
AND MODE OF DISTRIBUTION OUTSIDE IMMEDIATE FAMILY
IN INTESTACY LAWS FOR FIFTY STATES IN U.S.

Order of Inheritance by Spouse and Immediate Family	Mode of Distribution Outside Immediate Family	
	Division into Maternal and Paternal Moieties	Inheritance by Next of Kin
Spouse Given Priority over Immediate Family	8	16
Spouse Shares Part of Estate with Intestate's Parents*	3	7
Spouse Shares All of Estate with Intestate's Parents	1	15

*Spouse takes all of estate under a designated amount (e.g., $50,000 in Rhode Island) and one half of the remainder if the decedent leaves no descendants.
Gamma = .51.

the decedent's parents. Thus, adding the nearest-ancestor criterion to next-of-kin mode of distribution outside the immediate
family seems unrelated to the place of the spouse in intestacy
laws. The spouse's priority over the parents is related to the
distribution of estates outside the immediate family only where
the concept of paternal and maternal moieties is applied.

**Incestuous Marriage Prohibitions
and Next-of-Kin Provisions**

Chapter 1 described the intimate-kin group as consisting of
persons who, being the property of the same group, cannot be
exchanged for one another in marriage; i.e., marriage between
them is considered incestuous. Since material property is often
regarded as an extension of its owners, it is reasonable that there is
a connection between laws governing incestuous-marriage restrictions and intestacy laws pertaining to the distribution of estates
among kinsmen. Table 4–3 indicates the association between
mode of distribution of estates and kinds of incestuous-marriage
prohibitions. States using the concept of moieties tend to show a
somewhat higher rate of restriction of both first-cousin marriage
and marriage with certain affines (such as with parents-in-law).

TABLE 4–3 INCESTUOUS MARRIAGE PROHIBITIONS AND MODE
OF DISTRIBUTION OUTSIDE IMMEDIATE FAMILY
IN INTESTACY LAWS FOR FIFTY STATES IN U.S.

	Distribution Outside Immediate Family	
Incestuous-Marriage Prohibitions	Distribution by Maternal and Paternal Moieties	Next of Kin
First-Cousin Marriage*		
Prohibited	9	22
Permitted	4	15
Marriage Between Certain Affines**		
Prohibited	6	11
Permitted	7	26

*Gamma = .21.
**Gamma = .34. Affines generally included in prohibited range are parents-in-law.

The data in Table 4–3 are in accordance with the earlier discussion of moiety as signifying separate paternal and maternal descent categories; the first cousin as a child of the parent's sibling would fall into the same intimate-kin group as the decedent if their marriage is prohibited, and this arrangement would stress descent relationships beyond the nuclear family, all of which would be consistent with the moiety concept. However, the findings in Table 4–3 are *not* consistent with the characterization of the concept of moiety as implying a separateness of the spouse from parents-in-law. Although a minority of states restrict marriage to specified affines, there is still a greater tendency for those legal codes which use the concept of moiety in distributing estates to prohibit affinal marriage. The analysis in the following section, pertaining to the condition whereby the criterion of the closest ancestor influences priority of succession outside the immediate family, is intended to provide additional relevant information regarding the relationship between incestuous marriage and succession laws.

**Incestuous Marriage Prohibitions
and Nearest-Ancestor Preference**

As noted earlier, in some states in which the principle of priority to the genealogically closest kin holds in inheritance, a second criterion is introduced. This latter criterion holds that, given two equidistant collateral relatives, the relative whose common ancestor with the decedent is closer to the decedent is given preference. This second criterion implies that the lines of descent tend to be dispersed generation by generation—it suggests a treeing-out or branching-out effect. If the branching out of relatives from a common ancestor is analogous to the partitioning of the wealth of the kinship group, giving priority to the heir with the nearest common ancestor to the decedent will ensure the transmission of the estate down to the most recent generation with least dissipation of wealth. This criterion can then be regarded, in line with the legal-family model, as a means for maintaining the property of the descent "group" down to the most recent generation possible. In contrast, when only the degree of relationship is considered (as in the first criterion), the estate is partitioned among all kin of equal degree of kinship to the decedent, with persons of an older generation sharing equally with those of a younger generation. This latter procedure is consistent with the primary distinction between the nuclear-family unit and an undifferentiated kindred in the natural-family model.

The discussion in the preceding paragraph leads to the conclusion that incestuous marriage patterns in states using "next of kin" as the only criterion differ from those in states adding the nearest common ancestor as a second criterion in partitioning estates outside the immediate family. An examination of the data in Table 4–4 bears out this expectation. To a greater extent than those states which provide only for closest degree of kinship, states with the nearest-common-ancestor criterion tend to forbid first cousins from marrying but generally permit any affines to marry.[17] This finding supports the statement that the closer-ancestor criterion expresses the legal-family paradigm.

Findings with regard to both first-cousin and affinal-marriage restrictions are thus consistent on the whole with statements about natural- and legal-family models. If the principle of the nearest-ancestor preference is intended to insure the transmission of estates to persons in the most recent generations, then this mechanism functions to keep an inheritance as intact as possible within the descent unit. The operation of this principle is described in the following paragraph.

The mechanism of the nearest-ancestor preference is based on the fact that a first cousin is the closest relative *in the decedent's*

---

[17] For first-cousin prohibitions, gamma in Table 4–4 is .60; for affinal prohibitions, gamma is .51.

TABLE 4–4 INCESTUOUS-MARRIAGE PROHIBITIONS AND MODE
OF DISTRIBUTION OUTSIDE IMMEDIATE FAMILY
FOR THIRTY-SEVEN STATES IN WHICH DEGREE
OF RELATIONSHIP IS A BASIS
FOR INHERITANCE IN INTESTACY LAWS

Incestuous-Marriage Prohibitions	*When More Than One Person Is Next of Kin, Those Related to Decedent Through Nearest Ancestor Preferred*	*Next of Kin Is Only Criterion**
First-Cousin Marriage**		
Prohibited	13	9
Permitted	4	11
Marriage Between Certain Affines***		
Prohibited	3	8
Permitted	14	12

*Persons in closest degree of relationship to decedent share per capita.
**Gamma = .60.
***Gamma = .51. Affines generally included in prohibited range are parents-in-law.

generation outside the immediate family, and a grandparent is the nearest common ancestor to the decedent and any cousin. The decedent's uncles and aunts are of course the immediate heirs of the grandparent. As the children of these uncles and aunts, all first cousins are the direct beneficiaries of the estate, since they can inherit from their parents directly or from the grandparent per stirpes. In contrast, *all* other relatives are descended through the great-grandparents, or even more distant kin, and therefore are assigned a lower priority (even when degree of relationship is equal). Hence, with the grandparent as the closest common ancestor, first cousins serve as substitute siblings to receive the estate intact. It is then not surprising that prohibition of first-cousin marriage and the nearest-ancestor criterion in intestacy laws go together.

Summary of Findings on Modern Intestacy Laws

The findings so far in this chapter are as follows:
1. As a general principle, laws governing intestacy tend to resemble inheritance patterns where wills are made. Circum-

stances regarding need, personal services or obligations, and alienation produce modifications in testated inheritance.

2. States in which the spouse succeeds to the full estate (when there are no children) tend to use the conception of maternal and paternal moieties to a greater extent than do states in which the spouse shares the estate with the decedent's parents.

3. States using the concept of moieties generally are more restrictive in marriage between first cousins and between certain affines.

4. For states using the "next-of-kin" criterion, those which also give preference to the kinsman related through the closest common ancestor to the decedent tend to forbid first cousins from marrying but generally permit any affines to marry.

The laws relating to intestacy thus seem to follow general practices when wills are made. There is some evidence that inheritance laws and incestuous-marriage laws tend to conform to the configurations implied in the natural- and legal-family paradigms.

A HISTORICAL VIEW OF AMERICAN
INHERITANCE LAWS

American statutes pertaining to inheritance have their roots in European law. The influence of English common law is apparent in early legal codes of the eastern United States. This influence was felt not only in New England but in other states as well. For example, in early New York law, "distribution of the personality of a married woman, who died intestate leaving a husband surviving and no descendants, was not controlled by any statute of New York, but by the common law, under which her entire personal estate was vested in her husband by virtue of his marital rights. . . . Although the common-law rule, that males shall be admitted before females, had been superceded in certain cases [by 1893], yet it still obtained in cases of remote collateral kinship" even at that late date.[18]

Early statutes, however, were not merely legislative ratifications of English common law. As early as 1784, Tennessee law indicated marked departures from common law, whose features were "peculiar to . . . Great Britain, and founded in principles of the feudal system which no longer apply in the government and

---

[18] New York statutes, 1967, 4–1.1, p. 484.

can never apply in this state."[19] Bills to abolish entail and primogeniture in Virginia at the end of the eighteenth century were justified on ideological grounds as preventing the concentration of wealth in ways "which made one member of every family rich and all the rest poor."[20]

A second major influence on American law was the French Civil Code enacted under Napoleon. States borrowed sections of the French Code, which was the basic format for Louisiana law. Elements of the French Code appear currently in many state laws; for example, much of the California Code dealing with succession is taken directly from French-Louisiana law.

An important difference between English common law and the French Civil Code resides in the conceptions of marriage. English common law sees marriage as the fusion of two lines of descent, the creation of a new set of statuses of husband and wife in their spouse's family of orientation. Jurally, they become a single personality. On the other hand, marriage in the French Code connotes an alliance between two distinct lines whereby the husband and wife retain their identities as members of their natal descent units, By borrowing from both traditions, American law makers adapted the products of European experience to American requirements. Although some borrowing may have been done rashly, presumably the American statutes reflected conscious modifications to fit the ethnic, economic, and political institutions in the particular states. To the extent that the selection of codes from the common-law and civil-law traditions was judicious, it indicates an expression of the paradigm of kinship (whether or not the selection was explicit or conscious) which the legislators saw as most appropriate for their constituents. Therefore, presumably, the statutory conception of marriage as fusion or as alliance of descent units corresponded to the constituents' paradigms of kinship.

As in the analysis of contemporary laws pertaining to succession and inheritance, the basic kinship paradigm implicit in earlier legal codes is revealed in those statutes covering priorities and contingencies for situations in which the intestate decedent leaves no direct descendants. The following sections deal with inheritance by the surviving spouse and with sex differentiation in intestacy laws, particularly in relation to provisions made for kinsmen outside the nuclear family.

[19] Tennessee statutes, 1784 (Nashville: James Smith, 1836), Ch.22, p. 248.

[20] Keim, "Influence of Primogeniture and Entail."

Sex Differentiation in Inheritance and Succession

Both common-law and Roman traditions give priority to males in succession to the family estate. The "family" in these traditions is a corporate "individual." "Maine's analysis of 'The Early History of Property' in Chapter VIII of *Ancient Law,* turns on two propositions. The first is that early law recognizes persons only as members of 'families' as continuations of their forefathers and as antecedents of their successors . . . . The second proposition is that early law does not distinguish between the Law of Persons and the Law of Things . . . . Hence, early law is incapable of recognizing distinctions between classes of property . . . . In other words, it is status that determines control over property and not the class of property that confers status."[21] Thus, insofar as domestic authority and control are vested in males in the common-law and Roman conceptions of "family," responsibility for family property as a tool of this authority must also be extended to males.

Vesting control and proprietorship in the same male as "head" of the family places him in the role of entrepreneur. Since, like material wealth, family members are "family" property, his control is also vested over them. A long historical trend has existed to divest the family head of authority over the human and material property of the family. The decline of sex differentiation in American laws of succession can be viewed as a step toward the separation of ownership from control over family property in the legal-family paradigm.

Table 4–5 reviews laws pertaining to distribution within the immediate family in force over a century ago in the United States. The table includes the 44 states and territories for which statutes could be found (and interpreted). The earliest laws were enacted just after the Revolution, and except for the state of Washington's 1881 statutes, the latest in the table were passed in the Civil War period. Of the 44 state laws, 22 provided that the father be given priority over mother and siblings in transmission of estates where no descendants of an intestate decedent existed; in the other 22 statutes, both father and mother inherited jointly or equally. As Table 4–5 indicates, when fathers were given priority in the succession of estates, the mother tended to be grouped with the siblings of the decedent in that, when the father was dead, she shared the estate with her children. Sexual differentiation was

---

[21] Fortes, *Kinship and the Social Order,* p. 295.

TABLE 4–5 PRIORITY OF INHERITANCE IN IMMEDIATE FAMILY
(WHEN NO SPOUSE OR ISSUE) FOR PARENTS AND SIBLINGS
OF DECEDENT IN NINETEENTH-CENTURY INTESTACY LAWS
FOR FORTY-FOUR STATES AND TERRITORIES

Priority Between Mother and Siblings of Decedent	Priority Between Parents	
	Father Given Priority over Other Family Members	*Both Parents Inherit Jointly or Equally*
Mother shares estate jointly or equally with siblings	13	3
Mother not grouped with siblings in priority of distribution	9	19

Gamma = .80.

given priority over generational categories. Thus the father was in one class and the rest of the family in another. In statutes where both parents shared in the estate, however, generational differentiation provided the basis for partition of the estate, with the parents in one class and the siblings in a second class. Emphasis on the sexual dimension seems to have facilitated a conception of descent as a perpetual line of ancestors and descendants; emphasis on generational differences promoted a view of the unity of the marital pair, which is basic to the natural-family paradigm.

The relationship between paternal priority in intestate inheritance (where there are no descendants) and mode of distribution outside the immediate family in nineteenth-century law is shown in Table 4–6. Of the 22 statutes in which the father was given priority:

1. In seven, the distribution was to next of kin in equal degree without regard to particular genealogical relationship.

2. In nine statutes a second criterion was added, namely, that when several relatives were equidistant from the decedent, preference was given to the kinsmen related to him through the closest ancestor.

3. Three legal codes provided that the estate be divided into moieties, with paternal and maternal kin sharing equally.

4. And in three cases, when several persons were next of kin in equal degree, preference was given to paternal kinsmen. For example, the paternal grandfather (and those who inherit from

TABLE 4–6 PATERNAL PRIORITY IN INTESTATE INHERITANCE
(WHEN THERE ARE NO DESCENDANTS)
AND MODE OF DISTRIBUTION OUTSIDE IMMEDIATE
FAMILY FOR FORTY-FOUR STATES AND TERRITORIES
IN THE NINETEENTH CENTURY

Mode of Inheritance Outside Immediate Family (When No Spouse, Issue, or Immediate-Family Member Survives)	Priority of Inheritance in Immediate Family (When No Spouse or Issue)	
	Father Given Priority over Other Family Members	Both Parents Inherit Jointly or Equally
Next of kin in equal degree	7	14
Next of kin, but kin related through nearest ancestor to decedent given preference	9	1
Division of estate into paternal and maternal moieties	3	2
Enumeration of priorities among kin: grandfathers, grandmothers, uncles, aunts, and so on.	—	5
Next of kin, with preference for paternal kinsmen	3	—

Gamma computed for "Next of kin in equal degree" versus all other categories together is .58.

him per stirpes) was given preference over the maternal grandfather.

Of the 22 statutes in which both parents inherited jointly or equally, when there were no descendants or immediate-family members of the person dying intestate:

1. In most states (14), the estate was distributed to next of kin in equal degree.

2. Only one state provided that, when several kinsmen were of equal degree of distance from the decedent, the person related to the nearest ancestor be given priority.

3. The remaining seven statutes directed that the estate be divided into moieties for paternal and maternal kin. However, in five of these, moiety distribution held only for grandparents and those who inherited from them per stirpes; these states were governed essentially by a compromise between moiety and next-of-kin modes of distribution.

Table 4–6 shows that when provisions for distribution within the immediate family are compared with those for more distant kinsmen, the following results appear: in the 22 statutes in which fathers were given priority, *seven* provided for distribution among next of kin, whereas *fifteen* made provisions which emphasize lineal dimensions of kinship (that is, preference for kinsmen related through nearest ancestor, moiety, priority to paternal kinsmen). However, in those legal codes in which both parents inherited jointly or equally, *fourteen* provided for distribution among next of kin, and only *eight* utilized other provisions.[22] Hence, there is a clear indication that statutory preference for paternal inheritance within the immediate family is associated with forms of distribution stressing lineal genealogical relationships of more distant kinsmen rather than the integrity of the nuclear family.

Inheritance by Surviving Spouse

The divestment of control by the male family head is also seen in the trend during the nineteenth century toward full inheritance by spouses. Vestiges of entail, which is characteristic of the old English common law, were found in the practice of dower for widows (and *curtesy for widowers). Under dower, widows were assigned one-third lifetime interest in their husband's land. For example, Connecticut statutes published in 1786 provided for "One third Part of the personal Estate to the Wife of the Intestate (if any be) forever; besides her Dower, or Thirds in the Houses and Lands during Life, where such Wife shall not be otherwise endowed before Marriage . . . . And in case there be no Children, nor any legal Representatives of them, then one Moiety of the personal Estate shall be allotted to the Wife of the Intestate forever; and one third of the real Estate for Term of Life . . . . And the Widows Thirds or Dower in the real Estate, at the expiration of her Term, shall be also divided." Similar provisions appear in Illinois law, derived from the 1787 Northwest Ordinance, which in turn was modeled after the English Statute of Distribution of 1670.[23] Provisions of English statute persisted in modern Illinois law well into the twentieth century. In 1845, if the intestate died

---

[22] A gamma computed for this comparison is .58.

[23] Dunham, "Wealth Transmission at Death," pp. 257–258.

without close kin (i.e., kinsmen were more distant than parents), the surviving spouse was given all personal property and half the real estate outright. After a series of other revisions, by 1929 (except where the decedent's parents were heirs) distinctions between personal and real property were dropped. Finally, in 1959, when neither close kin nor spouse survived, a system was adopted to determine heirs through great-grandparents and their descendants.

The trend observed in Illinois law represents a continual shift in the status of the surviving spouse also found in other states. The spouse becomes increasingly independent from the decendent's family of orientation in relation to the family property. A Cook County study (in large part Chicago) indicated clearly that testators tended to will everything to their wives, thereby giving their wives wide discretion in managing and later devolving estates.

The growing independent status of the surviving spouse from her husband's (or his wife's) family of orientation is also apparent in the use of *trusts. In an analysis of wills drawn in Essex County, New Jersey during the nineteenth century, Friedman found a marked decrease in the use of trusts from 1850 to 1900.[24] In 1850 over seventy percent of the wills involved trusts and other non-outright bequests, but by 1900 the proportion dropped to forty percent. "Except in the case of minor children of either sex, trusts and life estates were almost exclusively for the benefit of women—the wife or daughter of the testator in most cases."[25] The creation of trusts, according to Browder, "permits an efficient and flexible means of transmitting property to minors, one that includes some assurance that their interests will be properly protected."[26]

In summary, historically the American practice has been an increasing separation of the interests of the surviving spouse from the decedent's family of orientation. The current practice in testation is to will the entire estate to the spouse and to permit it to devolve to the children upon the death of the widow (or widower). In this way, testators have come to provide their surviving spouses with a maximum of flexibility in the disposition of

[24] Lawrence M. Friedman, "Patterns of Testation in the 19th Century: A Study of Essex County (New Jersey) Wills," *American Journal of Legal History* 8 (1964), pp. 41–45.

[25] Ibid., p. 45.

[26] Browder, "Recent Patterns of Testate Succession," p. 1360.

estates.[27] The isolation of the interests of the surviving spouse from the decedent's family of orientation suggests that, in American society, marriage is losing its role to fuse together diverse families and their estates in succeeding generations (a role implied in the natural-family paradigm).

Geographical Region and Rules of Inheritance

Different patterns in statutes, as expressions of kinship paradigms, reflect contrasts in social conditions or composition of population among states and territories. The manner by which the United States was settled and its mode of expansion westward suggests the need for a comparison of early legal codes for states and territories east of the Mississippi River with those of states and territories west of the Mississippi. In large measure, eastern states were dominated by English settlers and their descendants; even the influx of other immigrants prior to the Civil War did not displace the English ethnic group in power, dominance, and authority. Migration to the territories west of the Mississippi did not generally diffuse some New England traditions; however, the western frontiers also exemplified escape from the constraining social structure built on Puritan foundations. It might then be expected that western American laws depart to some extent from English common-law traditions.

Indeed, laws pertaining to incestuous marriage in western America differ markedly from proscriptions in the East, particularly New England. As noted in Chapter 2, western American laws generally prohibit first-cousin marriage but permit any affines to marry. The preceding section of this chapter, dealing with current laws on inheritance, showed that these patterns of marital proscriptions are associated with tendencies in inheritance laws either (a) to give preference to kinsmen closest to the nearest common ancestor or (b) to divide the estate into paternal and maternal moieties (rather than merely to apportion estates among next of kin). It might be anticipated that century-old statutes giving priorities to the father would also tend to predominate west of the Mississippi River.

Table 4–7 indicates the historical regional distribution of laws in which the father is given priority in inheritance as compared with those in which both parents inherit equally and

---

[27]   Sussman, Cates, and Smith, *The Family and Inheritance*, pp. 126–128.

Family and Estate **109**

TABLE 4–7 ORDER OF PRIORITIES OF INHERITANCE AND
LOCATION OF STATE OR TERRITORY IN
NINETEENTH-CENTURY AMERICAN INTESTACY LAWS

Order of Priorities of Inheritance	Location of State or Territory	
	East of Mississippi River	West of Mississippi River
When No Spouse or Issue:*		
Father Given Priority Over Others in Immediate Family	10	12
Father and Mother Inherit Jointly or Equally	14	8
When No Member of Immediate Family (or Issue) Survives:**		
Next of Kin Only Criterion	17	4
All Other Modes of Distribution***	7	16

*Gamma = .36.
**Gamma = .81.
***Includes priority to kin related through nearest ancestor, distribution through maternal and paternal moieties, distribution through designated grandparents, and patrilineal preference.

jointly. Of the 22 states and territories which gave preference to the father in the nineteenth century, only *ten* were east of the Mississippi, whereas 14 out of the 22 states in which both parents inherit were in the east.[28] Table 4–7 also shows the regional distribution of laws providing for partitioning of estates outside the immediate family. Twenty-one states and territories provided for inheritance of estates by next of kin (without additional provisions); of these, 17 were east of the Mississippi River. However, of the 23 states and territories which provided for other arrangements (that is, division into moieties, preference to kinsmen closest to nearest common ancestor, or preference to paternal kin), only *seven* were east of the Mississippi.[29] Hence, historically, provisions for both parents and for next of kin to inherit tend to be found in the East where American Biblical incestuous-marriage prohibitions also occur (but not in the West). Consequently, the configuration of laws suggests that, while in the East the natural family paradigm tended to predominate, the seeds of the legal-family model were sown in western statutes.

[28] Gamma computed for this distribution is .35.

[29] Gamma computed for this distribution is .81.

CONCLUSION

Laws of inheritance and succession are further evidence of the diminished use of the natural-family paradigm as a basis for modern law. In states where incestuous-marriage laws tend to resemble Biblical proscriptions, inheritance laws generally fuse the spouse with the decedent's parents; this fusion symbolizes the integration of an individual into his spouse's family of orientation upon marriage. These states also assign priorities outside the nuclear family to next of kin without regard to the specific kind of relationship, the major distinction being nuclear family versus the kindred. Intestacy laws in states with Biblical-like incestuous marriage laws thus emphasize both affinal bonds and the unity of the nuclear family. This emphasis is consistent with the natural-family paradigm. In contrast, states which follow the western American pattern of incestuous-marriage laws are more consistent with the legal-family paradigm. In these states, the surviving spouse does not share the estate with the decedent's parents, but is treated separately and is given priority over them in case of intestacy. As for distribution outside the nuclear family, there is more emphasis in western American states on the use of moieties and on inheritance through the nearest ancestor (when two heirs are equidistant from the decedent). There is thus more separateness in the distinction of affinal versus consanguineal relatives; lines of descent are kept separate and given greater importance in the western American kinship system.

Modern statutes pertaining to distribution of estates reflect changes that have taken place in the course of American history. In the eastern part of the United States, nineteenth-century laws conformed to the natural-family paradigm, with (a) the decedent's parents sharing in the estate if there were no descendants, and (b) distribution outside the immediate family being to next of kin. In the West, however, there was greater stress on lineal descent: the father was given priority in case of intestacy, and the mother was relegated to sharing with siblings of the decedent; outside the nuclear family, moreover, maternal and paternal moieties and closest-ancestor provisions were introduced. With the advent of the twentieth century, although the provisions for sex differentiation in these statutes have disappeared, the accent on lineal descent in inheritance law remains. It is in the West, therefore, with its values of personal freedom and egalitarianism, that the foundations of the legal-family paradigm seem to have been laid.

The western American kinship paradigm seems to conform to

a different sort of economic model from that represented by the American-Biblical paradigm. The American-Biblical model stresses the fusion of families through marriage and a consequent minimizing of the importance of differentiating between maternal and paternal lines of descent or of specific genealogical ties. In economic terms, the American-Biblical model is one of consolidation of human and material capital by kinship groups in ways which might be useful in *achieving* greater power in the society. From the perspective of the whole society, the American-Biblical system provides a means for a continual consolidation of capital among wealthy families.

The western American system is different from the American-Biblical model, in that its system of marriage implies borrowing rather than exchanging spouses by families; the western American system is essentially a credit economy. Borrowing and lending suggests a temporary arrangement, retention of ownership rights by the natal family, and a failure of the affinal group to have a stake in the welfare of an individual who has married one of its members. Instead, families connected by marriage can have access to each other's services and resources without implication of political power or consensus on norms and values. Because of the temporary, tentative commitments between families, ruptures of relationships between them do not readily produce crises, and the probability of gross disequilibrium of the system is minimized. Hence, the western American system suggests a loosely coordinated system of social relationships in which there is neither political threat that demands strong alliances nor a basic consensus on moral and ethical codes that would dictate fusion of families.

There appears to be a relationship between modern economic structure and kinship paradigm. The natural-family paradigm was prevalent in American society at about the time of the American Revolution. A study of ownership of sea-going vessels in Salem, Massachusetts in 1800–1810 reveals a large number of family partnerships. Often organized informally, these partnerships not only served utilitarian purposes but also symbolized the persistence of family solidarity. The funds pooled as capital by relatives or friends, however, restricted the scope of commercial enterprises, and the stability of partnerships depended on family cohesion.[30] Similarly, a study of Jewish families in New York by

---

[30] Bernard Farber, *Guardians of Virtue: Salem Families in 1800* (New York: Basic Books, Inc., 1972), pp. 75–96.

Hope Leichter and William Mitchell also suggests a close relationship between partnership organization of business and kinship organization following Biblical lines.[31] Like the sharing of relatives implied in the natural-family paradigm, the family partnership creates a common fund to be shared by the participating relatives. Both kinship paradigms and partnership reflect a conception of cohesion in small groups through property sharing.

In contrast to the natural-family paradigm, the legal-family paradigm seems to suggest a different magnitude of economic organization. The legal-family model seems consistent with the concept of the industrial corporation. Modern industrial complexes make *use* of investment capital without affording any special managerial rights or obligations to the investors. Similarly, kinsmen organized in accordance with the legal-family model make *use* of each other's members—as investment capital—without giving the families related by marriage any managerial rights over affines. In the legal-family model, the term "in-law" merely refers to the spouse's relatives, without implying any special rights or obligations. In adoption, according to the legal-family paradigm, the adopting families obtain the exclusive managerial rights over the adopted child, without leaving the natural family, which produced the adoptee, any residual rights in the child. In inheritance, the legal-family model implies that the properties transmitted are investment capital, whose allocation is unrestricted. With an absence of controls over the recipient's use, the legal-family paradigm contrasts sharply with those models which have constraints on the disposition of inheritances; these constraints include the obligations of the patrician to his relatives in colonial America, the family council in France, or the legal entail of estates in England. In brief, the conception of the modern corporation as a legal personality is analogous to the definition of family and kinship relationships strictly as legal constructions. Both owe their very existence and rules to a state charter. Both the corporate personality and the familial lines of descent are seen as having a perpetual life (unlike the nuclear family). In these respects, the legal-family model may be viewed as the prototype of other institutions in the society. We are all resources of families and corporate bodies as subsections of the state.

Although the temptation is strong to elaborate upon the similarities between kinship and corporate ownership in the

---

[31] Hope J. Leichter and William E. Mitchell, *Kinship and Casework* (New York: Russell Sage Foundation, 1967), pp. 135–145.

United States, there is also a danger in overextending the analogy. My intentions here are merely to point out a common thread in the separation of ownership and control in both institutions and to suggest that this separation pushes modern government to expand its role in their regulation.

5

The Changing Family
in American Society

The preceding chapters have dealt with changes in American family law without giving much consideration to specific social and historical conditions which these changes reflect. Yet, if the interpretation of the shift in law is accurate, we should be able to observe trends in American society which the transformation from the "natural"-family paradigm to the legal-family paradigm expresses. This chapter will review some of the major currents of ideas and events which produced this transformation.

The "natural"-family model appears in its clearest form among the New England Puritans and their descendants. Borrowing from English ecclesiastical family law and especially from Old Testament Hebrews, the New Englanders molded norms and values of family life which have exerted a widespread influence on American society. The first part of the chapter will focus upon a New England community at the end of the eighteenth century as a relatively pure case for describing the configuration of norms and values associated with the "natural"-family paradigm.

It has become commonplace to attribute the emergence of the modern family to industrialization and urbanization. According to Talcott Parsons, "it is above all the presence of the modern occupational system and its mode of articulation with the family which accounts for the difference between the modern, especially American, kinship system and *any* found in nonliterate or even peasant societies."[1] Similarly, William J. Goode indicates that industrialization and urbanization apply pressure at crucial points to force change in traditional family structure toward the conjugal-family model.[2] Still, these descriptions by Parsons and Goode may overemphasize change and imply that little of the traditional family remains except its basic functions in the procreation and socialization of children. Historical analysis is necessary to indicate more precisely the extent to which change has occurred.

The latter part of the chapter will examine some of the major currents of ideas about the family which accompanied major social movements growing out of modern industrialization and urbanization. It will indicate how egalitarian movements attended the shift to the legal-family paradigm. In particular, the ideas about family life in Marxian writings will serve to show the affinity between egalitarianism and the legal-family paradigm.

PREINDUSTRIAL AMERICAN
FAMILY IDEOLOGY

Most textbooks dealing with the American family note the historical significance of Puritanism. Generally, they refer to the Puritans as providing a basic model out of which the modern American family has developed.[3] Some historians, like Edmund S. Morgan, claim that the Puritan system failed when the Puritans "allowed their children to usurp a higher place than God in their affection."[4] Still, many aspects of Puritan family organization persisted long after the decline of Puritan doctrine and its

[1] Talcott Parsons and Robert F. Bales, *The Family, Socialization and Interaction Process* (New York: The Free Press, 1955), p. 11.

[2] William J. Goode, *World Revolution and Family Patterns* (New York: The Free Press, 1963).

[3] Panos Bardis, "Family Forms and Variations Historically Considered," in *Handbook of Marriage and the Family*, Harold T. Christensen, ed. (Chicago: Rand McNally, 1964), pp. 403–461; Stuart A. Queen and Robert W. Habenstein, *The Family in Various Cultures* (New York: J. B. Lippincott, 1967); Ira L. Reiss, *The Family System in America* (New York: Holt, Rinehart and Winston, Inc., 1971), pp. 49–50; Bert N. Adams, *The American Family* (Chicago: Markham Publishing Co., 1971), p. 66; Clifford Kirkpatrick, *The Family as Process and Institution* (New York: Ronald Press, 1963), pp. 119–123; Robert R. Bell, *Marriage and Family Interaction* (Homewood, Ill.: Dorsey Press, 1971), pp. 24–43.

[4] Edmund S. Morgan, *The Puritan Family* (New York: Harper Torchbooks, 1966), p. 185.

assumptions pertaining to predestination. In fact, one writer has asserted, "the culture of Puritan New England had more to do with the shaping of our national culture than did that of any other colonial region or that of any subsequent immigrant group."[5]

Instead of presenting an amorphous picture of New England family life, I would like to describe family organization in a particular community which was Puritan in origin and remained relatively homogeneous ethnically until after 1800.[6] In a community of this type, the post-Puritan model of the family probably appears in its purest form.

Historically, as noted earlier, American society has had deep roots in New England tradition evolving out of Puritanism, which spread to the New World in the seventeenth century. As of 1800, the institutional life of Salem, Massachusetts resembled that of earlier Puritans in various ways. The Puritans had used their interpretations of ancient Hebrew social organization as a model for family and community. In doing so, they applied the prescriptions of conduct implied by the "natural" family as a basic social unit. In time, old Puritan families and their offshoots became the Federalist elite, and their ideas about family, economy, and government dominated the community, although institutional forms did vary considerably by socioeconomic status. It may be instructive to describe Salem family life of 1800 in some detail in terms of family government, wealth and family organization, political position and marital alliances, and socialization practices. This description may lend fuller understanding of the historical roots of current family ideology.

Family Government

In particular, the Puritans adhered closely to marriage and family practices found in the Bible. The head of the household was analogous to the patriarch, and the household members were under his authority. In early Puritan Salem, everyone had to live in a family and untested strangers were placed under the domestic

[5] Manford H. Kuhn, "American Families Today: Development and Differentiation of Types," in *Family, Marriage and Parenthood*, Howard Becker and Reuben Hill, eds. (Boston: D. C. Heath & Co., 1955), p. 134.

[6] Bernard Farber, *Guardians of Virtue, Salem Families in 1800* (New York: Basic Books, Inc., 1972) provides the basis for the ensuing discussion of family life in New England. That book is based mainly on the Historical Collections, diaries, and other publications of the Essex Institute in Salem, Massachusetts.

control of existing household heads. Those who refused to (or could not) conform to the codes established by the Elect were warned out of town. As late as 1790–1791, warnings were issued to roughly an eighth of the population, who were designated as Strangers, to leave Salem. Later records indicate that this warning did not rid the town of its poor population; yet the fact that such warnings were still given after the American Revolution reveals the persistence of Puritan community organization.

In the Salem of 1800 the importance of family government was still emphasized as a means of exerting social control over the young and the deviant. Children of the poor were placed into other families as apprentices in order to be raised "properly." Poor boys tended to spend most of their formative years in households other than their own. Removing young boys from poor families may have provided them with some means for upward social mobility, but it also deprived their families of additional earning power and kept these families in poverty. At the same time the long-term apprenticeships provided cheap labor for well-to-do artisan families. Often the artisans from poor families could not remain in the trade for which they had been trained but had to accept unskilled jobs. As apprentices, the poor were frequently shunted into the least remunerative and most overcrowded crafts. After their apprenticeships, they often lacked the tools, the capital, the degree of skill, and/or the health necessary to carry on as journeymen or as masters in their craft. In most instances, thus, the apprenticeship system inhibited upward social mobility of the lower-class youths and served thereby to maintain a dependent class, which generation after generation could be exploited under the apprenticeship system. As a result of such long-term apprenticeships, the concept of a semi-autonomous family government—a master ruling all those in his household domain—persisted long after the initial motivations for this arrangement had ceased.

Wealth and Family Organization

Family life in Salem varied among socioeconomic classes in the period 1790–1810. In the merchant class, there were numerous family partnerships. Marriage meant the symbolic incorporation of a person into his spouse's family of orientation; this symbolism created quasi-partnership bonds between sons- and brothers-in-law. The lone merchant who developed his enterprise independently of relatives and friends was unpopular. Although family solidarity among merchant families was highly valued, analysis of family partnerships in Salem of 1800 has indicated that, despite their symbolism of family solidarity, they were generally unstable. Apparently the competition for limited funds under a system of divided estates and the consequent potential for conflict among partners tended to break up families into smaller units.

For merchant families, an ambivalence existed between family solidarity and independence of nuclear families. On the one hand this solidarity strengthened their economic position in the community and contributed to the stability of their status. On the other hand, however, since their destiny was closely tied to that of their relatives, they were often committed to risks not of their own choosing, and thus they lacked flexibility in the use of capital.

Difficulties in merchant families developed not only in the relationships between partners but also in the inability of children to take over the family businesses. Numerous cases of suicide, mental illness, and homosexuality have been recorded among the children of strong patriarchal merchant-fathers. Often, too, the many heirs were unable to maintain a sense of solidarity sufficient to overcome conflicting interests or personal differences. While an effective division of labor could on occasion be established among the partners for a limited period of time, in the end the family partnership broke up, with the various members going their own ways. Thus family partnerships—particularly between heirs—despite their symbolism of solidarity and despite their maintenance of family resources, appeared to be inherently fragile.

The artisan class in Salem faced a different situation. The system whereby sons were apprenticed to relatives fostered family relationships markedly different from the participation of heirs in business as partners. Family partnerships depended upon sharing a finite amount of capital, organizing a division of labor, and developing a sense of solidarity to utilize this capital effectively. The family apprenticeship, however, depended upon the transmission of skills in service or manufacturing. Since, unlike capital, skill is not a finite commodity, the number of apprentices did not diminish skills, but actually increased the family standard of living.

Based on inheritance of skills rather than money, the degree of family solidarity among artisans in Salem was related to the degree of skill of the family craft. As a form of family property, the craft seemed to create a guild-like organization within the kinship group. Family solidarity between the male relatives was then, like the patriarchal Judaic tribe, the mechanism by which a strong web of kinship was maintained. With the development of the large-scale factory system in the United States, however, a craft system based on family apprenticeships could not persist as a competing institution. Consequently the strong ties between male relatives, which formed the basis of kinship network under the apprentice-ship system, could not endure. Still, some of the norms guiding entrepreneurial and artisan families in the Salem of 1800 do seem to be present in American society today, and these will be discussed later in the chapter.

Political Position and Marital Alliances

The form of family and community organization which derived from economic relationships between families also affected marital alliances. These alliances were often used by powerful families to maintain political control in the family. Various families sent representatives to both houses of Congress, to the Supreme Court, and to cabinet posts, and in addition, they were active in state and local government.

In general our analysis indicates that the various socio-economic strata utilized marriage differently. In the merchant class, families formed marital alliances to develop coalitions to sustain political power. These alliances involved different kinds of cousin marriage—particularly between *parallel cousins—and sibling exchange. The strong partisanship of family alliances militated against the creation of a unified upper class. Instead the constant power struggles between Federalist and Republican families made it easy for factions to form. These factions split the merchant and professional class not only in politics but also in social and economic activities. In the early nineteenth century, factional strife made possible significant shifts in political power.

The marital alliances created in the Salem artisan class served a different purpose from those in the merchant class. Among the artisans, these alliances—as evidenced by the pre-ponderance of cousin marriages with an uncle's daughter—enhanced solidarity among male consanguineal relatives. They strengthened family bonds and enabled the apprenticeship sys-tem to remain closely tied to kinship.

The weakness of the marital bond in the lower class created much discontinuity in family life and made political and economic efforts in that class ineffective.[7] The precariousness of marriage was merely another indication of the uncertainty of existence in the lower class of Salem. *Matrifocality, divorce, and desertion were associated with the "lowest vices" and, by contrast, the dominant role of the male and strong marriage ties in artisan and merchant families were valued as providing stability and certainty to family life.

Socialization in the Salem Family

There is some conflict over interpretations given by historians to socialization practices in the post-Puritan family. Some historians have emphasized the rigorous discipline in childrearing, while others have pointed to the presence of congeniality, amusements, and games. The contrary interpretations in bringing up children seem to result from a norm, apparently implicit in the Puritan tradition, which can be formulated as follows: Whatever does not interfere with one's general or particular calling is permitted. Consequently, complete self-denial would not be as necessary in high socioeconomic status families as in others. Election in these families had already been "demonstrated." This norm makes understandable the laws in the seventeenth century permitting the wealthy and other highly respected families to wear fancy clothes, to live in elaborate houses, to eat expensive food or to engage otherwise in conspicuous consumption, and to carry on discreet extramarital or premarital sexual liaisons without being accused of gross impiety. These acts, which would be regarded with horror among the poor and artisan classes, were instead signs of success among the affluent. If this norm was not readily apparent in the early Salem settlement, by 1790–1810 its signs could be recognized. The moderation in childrearing, especially for high socioeconomic status families, is indicated by interpretations of Salemites in 1790–1810 of deviant behavior as resulting from either excessive indulgence by parents or too harsh discipline

Artisans' families were held to strict discipline. The very structure of the apprenticeship system was based on authority and the development of self-discipline. This discipline involved the general practice whereby children, regardless of their familial

[7] Cf. Peter Kunstadter, "A Survey of the Consanguine or Matrifocal Family," *American Anthropologist* 65 (1963), pp. 56–66.

connections, often lived with families other than their own either as apprentices or as students. The custom of placing children in other families had existed in England before the seventeenth century and was justified on the grounds that children who are brought up in a home other than their own learn better manners. Affection by parents was considered to be inimical to the creation of discipline in children, and in preadolescence the children were already occupied with work and study. The asceticism which characterized the early American Puritan community seemed to have survived after the Revolution in artisan families and promoted their upward social mobility.

In brief, socialization in merchant-class families, while demanding some discipline, provided for considerable freedom of expression. Impulse control was not considered essential in these families. When deviance occurred, it did not generally take the form of acting out repressed impulses. Rather, deviance in merchant families involved the performance of immoral acts—love affairs, embezzlement, various kinds of indiscretions. In the artisan class, however, socialization entailed considerable discipline. Deviance often took the form of suppressed anger and hostility and of autistic behavior—complete withdrawal from society, moodiness, ennui. This is the class which seemed to be the major bearer of the "Protestant Ethic."

Salem Families: Some Implications

To summarize, the "natural-family" model of Salem prescribed certain patterns of conduct in family government, economy, and political life and served to integrate community relationships into a tight social system. Imbedded in Biblical law, the "natural-family" model in New England was based on rigorous control of family government, the apprenticeship system, and networks of political-familial alliances. Apparently because of the control mechanisms, the socialization practices and ethical standards associated with the Puritan family were able to survive long after the religious fervor faded away.

Central to the Salem family paradigm was the conception that the family was *the* basic building block of social order. In early Salem, only persons in families had full status as "inhabitants" of the community with full economic, social, and political rights. Since society consisted of family commonwealths, effective family government was necessary, with the family head responsible to town government for the conduct of his household. Given this responsibility, the family head had to hold authority over all aspects of the lives of his family, and the socialization of children called for the suppression of deviant impulses. Each member had to adhere to his family role, and family and marital ties had to be considered as permanent; otherwise the system could not work. The natural-family ideology dominated the entire community; it was a matter of situation and power that family life varied by socioeconomic status. This was the social background of New England family law.

THE POST-REVOLUTIONARY AMERICAN FAMILY

The "natural-family" model derived from Puritanism and based on Biblical injunctions was diffused throughout the United States following the Revolution. As New England ports became obsolete through the development of large ships, the more prosperous merchants and their families migrated to such commercial centers as New York. Artisans and unskilled workers traveled southward and westward as well. As a consequence, the Biblical-based family model was incorporated into the legal structure outside the East. As late as the mid-nineteenth century, Illinois marriage law followed Levitical norms. According to a footnote in the 1856 edition of Illinois Statutes of a General Nature (p. 739), "Under the statute of 1819, males of the age of seventeen and females of fourteen, could be joined in marriage, 'if not prohibited by the laws of God.' 'A.' married the daughter of his sister, and the marriage was held to be within the Levitical degrees, and voidable, though not absolutely void." In other state laws, such as the Michigan statutes of 1857 (Vol. II. p. 950), marital proscriptions followed the Levitical code although no Biblical reference was mentioned.

With industrialization and large-scale European immigration, people adapted their households to conform with the requirements of their work and with traditional community expectations, which were generally formulated by the old elite, often of New England ancestry. Family adaptations to migration and work were reflected in the greater participation of women in the factory throughout their lifetime, isolation from relatives, increase in divorce and desertion, rise in juvenile delinquency, and a decline in patriarchal control in the family. These changes have been described as "family disorganization," "family problems," and "decay of the family."

The application of such terms as "family disorganization" to trends in family life implies that the basic cultural model has remained the same but that there has been a decline in the extent to which actual behavior conforms to the set of ideal norms and values. To some sociologists, this discrepancy represents a *strain* which results from the increase in specialization of the family in industrial society.[8] A widening discrepancy between a traditional family model and actual behavior is considered as "moral decay."[9]

When one considers only the natural-family paradigm and ignores the emerging legal-family model, deviations from norms associated with the natural family are indeed "moral decay." In the so-called progressive era at the turn of the twentieth century, it was common to regard the effects of poverty, European immigration, rapid urbanization, and large scale industrialization as evidence of the general decay of moral standards in America. The phrase *moral decay* has an archaic ring to it today; too much has happened during the twentieth century to think that one set of standards will decay without others coming into existence to replace it. The remainder of this chapter is devoted to a discussion of the historical events and trends related to the emergence of current family paradigms.

In modern society, war and depression are ever threatening historical events which imperil traditional family norms and values. Wartime is associated with departures from routinized ways of doing things. The total mobilization of society to wage war necessitates changes in actual behavior, but not in ideal family models. Women work in defense plants, young men interrupt their careers to enter the military forces or to participate otherwise in the war effort. Many changes in family life connected with "moral decay" occur—hasty marriages are made, there is much promiscuity, couples move away from their relatives because of work or military commitments, wives are left alone at home while their husbands may be gone for months or even years. Thus in World War I and, in particular, in World War II, there were many departures in behavior from the traditional Puritan family model.

[8]   Parsons and Bales, *The Family, Socialization and Interaction Process.*

[9]   Raymond Firth, "Family and Kinship in Industrial Society," *The Sociological Review,* Monograph No. 8 (1964), p. 66.

Yet, while wars may weaken commitments to traditional cultural models, they do not produce ideologies of social structure which embody new family models. But economic depressions, on the other hand, may be capable of stimulating the production of new models. In families with unemployed fathers during the 1930's, paternal prestige and authority declined. This shift was particularly profound in families where mothers or children became the primary breadwinner. In the depth of the 1930's Depression, children of unemployed fathers tended to be more critical of them than did children of fathers who were working. This was especially the case if the mother was also critical of the father. The hardships of the Depression affected the family in other ways as well—crude marriage, birth, and divorce rates declined; children stayed in school longer; and there was an increase in illegitimacy rates.[10] Although some of these effects can be interpreted as strengthened family relationships (e.g., lower divorce rates), the weight of evidence is a worsening of the quality of family life. While crude divorce rates declined significantly, the amount of desertion, unrecorded in any official files, may have more than compensated for this decline. Actually, the rate of divorce per 1000 existing marriages did remain fairly high throughout the Depression. Paul Jacobson suggests, in addition, that welfare assistance and relief work projects favored men with families and deterred divorce. After the most severe depression period had passed, the divorce rate resumed its rapid rise, and Jacobson concludes that the early decline in divorce "concealed a host of disillusionment, friction, and bitterness."[11]

In general, the Depression shook the confidence of people in their basic institutions, including the family, and there was a significant deviation in family behavior from the norms associated with the traditional American model. The deviation was in many ways more pronounced than that associated with wartime; both young and established families alike were greatly affected as the economic and social stability of the older generation also declined. One question which may therefore be asked is: Did this departure from Puritan-derived family norms stimulate the emergence of new family models?

The characteristics of the contemporary American family

[10] Samuel A. Stouffer and Paul F. Lazarsfeld, *Research Memorandum on the Family in the Depression* (New York: Social Science Research Council, 1937), Bulletin No. 29.

[11] Paul H. Jacobson, *American Marriage and Divorce* (New York: Holt, Rinehart & Winston, Inc., 1959), pp. 95–96.

bear some resemblance to the preindustrial norms of family government, relationships to the economy, marriage, and socialization practices. There has been little change in the past century in the tendency for extended families to live together. For example, U.S. Census data for the 1850–1860 decade consistently show few grandchildren and grandparents living in the same household. Thus, it may be concluded that three-generation, extended households were virtually as exceptional in the mid-nineteenth century as they are today.[12]

With regard to family government, studies of juvenile delinquency, mental illness, and other forms of deviance ascribe to the family the blame of the failure of its members to develop into responsible citizens in the community. The ideal of domestic control still dominates the thinking of most political leaders and educators. There appears to be a general consensus that the poor and their children are incompetent to manage their affairs; social workers, counselors, and other agents of the welfare institution of the society are then brought in to assist them.

Wealth appears to play a similar but diminished role in family organization now as compared with the 1790–1810 era. Studies of leading families, however, suggest that in many instances (as in Salem's peak years as a seaport) family solidarity, although highly valued, may be difficult to maintain, and partnerships may be unstable.[13] Although considerable similarity exists between current and past entreprenurial families, the artisan class has declined. Since the artisan class rests heavily on strong ties between males, its passing has been accompanied by the weakening of kinship bonds between male relatives. However, the development of professional traditions in various families— medicine, university teaching, law, government service—marks the maintenance of these male kinship bonds among some professional groups. Although these groups may not be numerically dominant, they have used these traditions to maintain a fairly high socioeconomic position in society.

In political life, as in economic life, the Puritan-based family model seems to play a persistent though slowly declining role in contemporary society. While cousin marriage and sibling ex-

---

[12] Papers by Lawrence Glasco, Michael Katz, Stuart Blumin, and Tamara Hareven on family life during the nineteenth century in American cities presented at the Clark University conference on The Family, Social Structure, and Social Change, April 27–29, 1972, These papers show a marked similarity in this respect.

[13] Stephen Birmingham, *"Our Crowd," the Great Jewish Families of New York* (New York: Harper and Row, 1967).

change no longer provide a basis for forming factions, there is still a tendency for marriage to retain a political homogeneity in the upper reaches of the society. Kinship factors continue to figure strongly in upper class alliances, with the impact of symbolic aspects of kinship decreasing as the lower depths of society are reached. Here, consensual marriage, matrifocality, and high rates of divorce and desertion are found. Whereas ties with paternal kin figure strongly in the upper classes, maternal ties count in the lower classes.

The role of the family in contemporary social structure is suggested in the kinship terminology used by middle and lower socioeconomic groups to address in-laws. A study of kinship in a midwestern community indicates that middle-class young adults address their in-laws as "mother" and "father" when they feel close to them but address them by their first name when they feel more distant. The reverse is true for low socioeconomic classes, with the first name being used to indicate a close tie. This usage of kin terms of address implies that middle-class adults (regardless of motivation) recognize the status which they acquire in their spouse's family of orientation. This status is the equivalent to that of their spouse's and is an important aspect of their relationship to their in-laws. For the lower class, however, kinship ties formed with affines represent merely formal relationships, whereas the *real* ties of married couples with in-laws are personal. As personal ties, the lower-class relationships with in-laws do not depend so much upon marriage status as they do on ways people relate to their in-laws as individuals. Hence, for the lower class, marital ties are not the gateway to a symbolic incorporation into one's spouse's family of orientation; rather, as in the old Salem lower class, marital ties are relatively insignificant.[14]

In keeping with other aspects of family life, there appears to be some carry-over of the Puritan-based model in areas of socialization of children. In upper-class socialization, there is apparently emphasis upon moderation in childrearing; there is no attempt to inculcate strong motives of upward social mobility. For the middle classes, however, achievement motivation seems to be strong. In this class, there is much emphasis upon delayed gratification patterns, the suppression of eroticism which might interfere with achievement, and the recognition that effective authority (rather than a laissez-faire parent-child relationship)

---

[14] Bernard Farber, *Kinship and Class, A Midwestern Study* (New York: Basic Books, Inc., 1971).

should exist. In the lower class, there is less emphasis upon delayed gratification, repression of eroticism, and the development of effective authority patterns. Thus the general patterns in socioeconomic variations in the Salem family seem to have persisted into modern urban society.

There still remains the question: Just how much do norms governing the contemporary family resemble those which pertain to family government, economic and political activity, and patterns of socialization in the Salem family of 1790-1810? The next section will respond to this query.

CONTEMPORARY FAMILY MODELS

As suggested earlier in this chapter, most textbooks and theoretical discussions of American family attribute its emergence in contemporary form to urbanization and industrialization. Increases in the frequency of divorce since midcentury suggest profound changes in family organization, changes which have been reflected in the revision of laws discussed in previous chapters.

Divorce rates in the United States have varied considerably in the past half century. From 8.0 per thousand married women in 1920, the rate dropped to 6.1 in 1932–1933. Since the Depression years, however, ignoring the brief upsurge and peaking after World War II, there has been a general increase in divorce, reaching 9.6 in 1963 and 12.5 in 1968.[15] As of 1967, "about 15 percent of the men, and 17 percent of the women, under 70 years of age who had ever married had been divorced" at one time or another during their lifetime.[16] However, since the probability of divorce is highest in the early years of marriage, most of the adult population had passed its period of maximum risk at a time when divorce rates were low. Data collected by the U.S. Public Health Service indicate that while marriage rates for 1969–1971 have stabilized at around 10.7 per 1000 population, divorce rates have continued to increase.[17] "Between 1967 and 1968 the [crude] rate

[15]   U.S. Public Health Service, "Births, Marriages, Divorces, and Deaths for 1968," *Monthly Vital Statistics Report* 17 (March 12, 1969), No. 12.

[16]   Paul C. Glick and Arthur J. Norton, "Frequency, Duration, and Probability of Marriage and Divorce," *Journal of Marriage and the Family* 33 (1971), p. 309.

[17]   U.S. Public Health Service, "Births, Marriages, Divorces, and Deaths for February 1972," *Monthly Vital Statistics Report* 21 (April 24, 1972), No. 2.

increased from 2.6 to 2.9 [per one thousand resident population], an increase of 12 percent."[18] The rate climbed to 3.3 in 1969, 3.5 in 1970, and up to 3.7 in 1971.[19] Given this trend of a rising divorce rate, the 15–20 percent estimate of persons who have been married and then divorced at least once seems an understatement.

The Companionship Family

The institutional arrangements evolving from the Puritan ethic, and based for the most part upon Biblical social organization, may still dominate many norms and values of American family life. Yet, in the past half-century a counter-ideology of the family seems to be developing. This ideology has been called by various names, such as "democratic" or "companionship" families. Burgess, Locke, and Thomes write:

> The ideal construct of the family as a companionship would focus on the unity which developed out of mutual affection and intimate association of husband and wife and parents and children. . . . The modern democratic family approximates most nearly the ideal construct of the companionship family, in which the members enjoy a high degree of self-expression and at the same time are united by the bonds of affection, congeniality and common interests. . . . The American family is moving towards the companionship type of family, which may be described as follows: (1) Affection is the basis for its existence; (2) husband and wife have equal status and authority; (3) major decisions are by consensus; and (4) common interests and activities coexist with division of labor and individuality of interests.[20]

In Burgess' analysis, the opposite of the companionship family as an ideal construct was the institutional family. His conception of the institutional family was a conglomerate of characteristics of the Puritan family, the Chinese extended-family

---

[18]   U.S. Public Health Service, "Births, Marriages, Divorces, and Deaths for June 1969," *Monthly Vital Statistics Report* 18 (August 26, 1969), No. 6.

[19]   U.S. Public Health Service, "Births, Marriages, Divorces, and Deaths for December 1971," *Monthly Vital Statistics Report* 20 (February 28, 1972), No. 12.

[20]   Ernest W. Burgess, Harvey J. Locke, and Mary M. Thomes, *The Family, from Institution to Companionship* (New York: American Book Co., 1963), pp. 3–4.

system, and other patriarchal forms. However, Burgess did not extend his analysis of family types to the role these institutions play in sustaining (or minimizing) social stratification In the Salem of 1800, a close relationship existed between Puritan-based family norms and the maintenance of social stratification. In order that the Puritan-derived society persist, it was necessary for family norms to emphasize (a) the authoritarian relationship between parents and children, (b) the influence of parents upon the marriage of their children, (c) prudence and family duty as values, and (d) the close connections between familial, political, and economic activities.[21] In Burgess' conception of the institutional family, the role of property in determining family organization is particularly strong.

Aside from its use in the analysis of contemporary family life, the Burgess conception of the companionship family is significant in its similarity to Engels' description of the proletarian family in the nineteenth century.[22] (This similarity does not of course imply agreement in political beliefs.) Engels speculated that in the post-capitalistic era which would eventually evolve to a communist society, the proletarian family would serve as a model. This family was characterized by its independence from property rights, equal rights for women, and persistence only through the mutual consent of husband and wife. Superimposition of Burgess' ideal construct of the companionship family upon Engels' conception of the proletarian family suggests the possibility that we can view Marxian family ideology as an archetype of family norms associated with an egalitarian social movement.

The Marxian Family Model

There has been considerable disagreement over exactly what Karl Marx and Frederick Engels regarded the destiny of the family to be as an institution in socialist society. Although one common interpretation is that they envisioned the complete elimination of the family, another is that Marx and Engels considered the family as a necessary but subordinate element in historical development. At any rate, one of the major features of the Marxian position is its rejection of the concept of "natural family" as a factor in social

[21] Farber, *Guardians of Virtue.*

[22] Frederick Engels, *The Origin of the Family, Private Property, and the State* (New York: International Publishers, 1942), pp. 70–73.

organization. It clearly separates the biological aspects of procreation from the form of family organization. Instead, Marx and Engels regard traditional European family structure to have derived from the economic division of labor by sex and the exploitation of women by men.

In essence, because of their emphasis upon division of labor and power relationships, Marx and Engels view patterns of exchange as the foundation of family organization. If a particular family form fails to produce self-realization for each human personality, the reason for that failure is that the family form is based upon domination and exploitation rather than free negotiation among family members. Marx and Engels contemplated the withering away of (at least) the exploitative bourgeoisie family form in a socialist world. Hence, in the Marxian view, there are neither "natural-family" norms or functions; rather, the form of the family in an epoch is the product of historical forces.[23]

Some distinctions can be drawn between the Puritan-based model and the companionship-proletarian model. The Puritan-based model postulates a crystallized division of labor (particularly important in support of the apprenticeship system in New England), sharp role differentiation by sex and age, an emphasis on paternal authority, and an orientation toward the familial accumulation of productive property. The companionship-proletarian model emphasizes minimal division of labor, flexible role arrangement which tends to disregard age and sex, egalitarianism, and personal happiness. As an ideal construct, it has the following goals:

1. *Egalitarian ideal.* This goal affects both interaction among family members and the relationship of the family to social structure. Within the family, lack of control over productive property, according to the ideology, removes the power base needed for patriarchal authority. In relation to social structure, the elimination of the property foundations of the family precludes inequality of occupational opportunity and eliminates economic consideration from courtship and marriage. Because marital alliances lose their utility in social stratification, the social position and personal characteristics of affines also decline in importance.

2. *Opposition to exploitation.* Associated with egalitarianism is the devaluation of exploitation. The Puritan family stimulated its members to show their state of election to grace by hard

[23] See also Erich Fromm, *Marx's Concept of Man* (New York: Frederick Ungar, 1966), pp. 201–206.

work and self-discipline; Marxian family ideology implies a need for a form of family organization which is voluntaristic so that people do not face exploitation in family relationships. In relationship to the community, proletarian family ideology also differs from the Puritan concept of family government, with its basis in the apprenticeship system, which justifies exploitation of the young, the poor, and the unskilled.

3. *Collective security.* In reaction to the possible exploitation of the powerless, the family in Marxian ideology emphasizes collective security. The stress upon mutual affection and maintenance of self-esteem signifies the importance of the family for emotional security. Its persistence as a voluntary collectivity implies, among other things, a haven from the demands of other groups.

Some writers, consistent with the Marxian view, suggest that since the incest taboo is central to the nature of family organization, as the family withers away, there will be no reason to prohibit sex relations among closely related persons, even between mother and son. Shulamith Firestone writes that "even if he should happen to pick his own genetic mother, there would be no *a priori* reasons for her to reject his sexual advances, because the incest taboo would have lost its function. The 'household,' a transient social form, would not be subject to the dangers of inbreeding."[24] Thus extreme interpretations of the Marxian position (as exemplified in writings of the women's liberation movement) contemplate not merely a reallocation of functions of procreation and socialization, but also the destruction of the nuclear family *in whatever form* as a necessary goal in revolutionizing society.

DIFFUSION OF MARXIAN NORMS

The attempt to draw a connection between nineteenth-century Marxism and twentieth-century family organization in the United States is fraught with the same kinds of difficulties faced by Weber in trying to relate early Protestantism and modern capitalism. First, there are ideologies, similar but not identical with Marxism, which have been important in American life. For the most part, American labor movements were influenced by Marxists and were sometimes a response to Marxian ideology.

[24] Shulamith Firestone, *The Dialectic of Sex* (New York: Morrow, 1970).

The non-Marxian ideologies seem comparable to the non-Puritan ascetic sects and denominations in Weber's *The Protestant Ethic* in terms of their imperfect approximations of the central ideology. Second, forms of family life similar to the one described by Engels have appeared at other times and places. Usually, however, these family forms were regarded as signs of "moral decay." Most often they were regarded as the result of the inability of families to conform to the most preferred manner of family life. Conformity to the proletarian-companionship family form, when it occurred in the nineteenth century, was an adaptation to such conditions as poverty, migration, sparse settlement, or personality problems which separated families and undercut the foundations of authority.

Changes in twentieth-century America seem, however, to be of a different quality. Until the Russian Revolution, Marxian ideology was closely identified with particular socialist, communist, and social democratic movements. After the Revolution, however, issues with which Marxism dealt began to reach wider publics. Various factors may be responsible for this diffusion—the spread of industry, the influx of Europeans sophisticated in political theory, the increase in literacy, and the existence of the USSR as part of the world reality. As long as Marxism remained a "dream," the issues it raised were only theoretical; as symbolized in the USSR (however inaccurate), the foundations of Marxism had to be taken seriously. The strong stances taken in reaction for or against the political and economic policies of the USSR served to educate the American public—particularly those disenchanted with American society. After World War I, many young people rebelled against traditional family organization, which had developed from a Puritan base. The rebellion, however, required not only urbanization, but also other conditions to transform American family models. These other conditions included, aside from secularization of society, (a) changes in family consumption patterns and (b) subordination of family to bureaucracy.

Family Consumption Patterns

Perhaps the greatest impetus toward the diffusion of Marxian family ideology occurred during the Great Depression. At this time families rooted in the Puritan tradition found themselves powerless to maintain their economic welfare. Collective security was recognized in industrial unions. Social security in old age was established as a right. Major appeals to voters and public opinion in general were based upon the right of "freedom from want."

Since the Depression, the American family has been veering away from accumulating capital through personal savings and investment, which are highly valued in the Puritan-based model, toward disposing income immediately and relying on health insurance and pensions to deal with crises and retirement. This trend is apparent in changes in the amount of money in savings and securities as compared with pension funds and installment consumer credit.

With 1950 as a base (i.e., index number of 100), the relative growth of personal savings and security investments versus pension reserves and consumer credit in installment purchases is shown in Table 5–1. Only installment consumer credit is considered in this analysis in order to differentiate between that credit which extends beyond short-term personal income and that which is used for convenience. The data reveal that whereas the cumulative amount of money in savings and securities trebled from 1950 to 1967 (index numbers 312 for savings, and 309 for securities), pension funds and consumer credit increased much more rapidly. The amount in private pension funds in 1967 rose about tenfold over that in 1950; the funds in government pension funds quadrupled; while the monies involved in installment credit increased over fivefold. At the same time, annual disposable personal income rose in an amount closer to that of investments in savings and securities than the amount involved in pension reserve and consumer credit; the increase in disposable personal income rose only 2.64 times from 1950 to 1967.

The tendency for increases in consumer credit and pension reserves to outstrip rises in savings and investment suggests a movement away from "the Protestant ethic," which emphasizes personal success through continual reinvestment of capital. That ethic demands that disposable income be diverted to savings and then to investment rather than to immediate consumption. Various trends have emerged in American society since World War II which contribute to the erosion of the ethic. Continual inflation makes delay of purchases costly. Generally, through the use of credit cards for long-term loans and easy availability of a wide variety of services and commodities, there is a constant temptation to fulfill wants immediately and to raise one's standard of living. Moreover, attractive packaging and convenience in purchasing through discount houses and shopping centers facilitate

TABLE 5–1 RELATIVE GROWTH OF DISPOSABLE PERSONAL INCOME, SAVINGS, AND SECURITIES HOLDINGS BY INDIVIDUALS, PENSION RESOURCES, AND INSTALLMENT CONSUMER CREDIT, WITH 1950 AS BASE FOR INDEX NUMBERS

Index Numbers

Year	Disposable Personal Income	Individuals' Savings	Securities Held by Individuals	Private Pension Reserves	Government Pension Reserves	Installment Consumer Credit
1950	100	100	100	100	100	100
1955	133	132	161	242	150	197
1960	169	175	205	467	228	293
1961	176	—	—	—	—	299
1962	186	207	219	575	267	331
1963	196	227	252	650	289	378
1964	212	250	279	733	317	427
1965	229	273	299	817	344	485
1966	247	284	270	833	372	527
1967	264	312	309	859	400	544
1968	285	—	—	953	—	612
1969	305	—	—	—	—	669

Installment Consumer Credit does not include mortgages or ordinary charge accounts. Disposable Personal Income refers to residual income after deduction of personal taxes against income, property, and individuals.

Sources: Economic Statistics Bureau of Washington, D.C., *The Handbook of Basic Economic Statistics,* 1969, Vol. 23, No. 3, p. 158, and January, 1971, Vol. 25, No. 1, p. 237; *Statistical Abstract of the United States,* 1969, pp. 453 and 460, and 1970, pp. 290 and 451.

spending. Besides, people are constantly urged through sophisticated television advertising to enjoy life *now* and to believe that almost any commodity is within one's reach. This constant urging and facilitation of spending devalues asceticism, the development of delayed gratification patterns in personality and the tradition of self-discipline in consumption patterns.[25] The scale of major commercial and industrial enterprise is now too large for control by individual families. The ideal of the rising patrician family is no longer feasible, and consequently middle-class families do not encourage their members to orient their resources toward enterprise or to delay or sacrifice personal gratification. Under these conditions, motivation toward the accumulation of capital investments is dissipated, and property no longer exists (except possibly in already wealthy families) as a basis for family organization.

Family and Bureaucracy

In its emphasis on humanism, Marxism distinguished between affluence and power. It was concerned primarily with problems of exploitation, alienation, and powerlessness; the "new middle class," despite its affluence, is rendered powerless by the giant bureaucratic organization of modern society.[26] As in the proletarian family, a sense of powerlessness probably makes the bureaucratic family amenable to family forms associated with permissiveness and equalitarianism. Miller and Swanson have indicated a relationship between employment of parents in bureaucratic settings and emphasis on permissiveness, warmth, and friendliness in childrearing.[27] In this sense the "new middle class" offers a direct threat to the system of norms and values associated with Puritanism. This situation would facilitate the diffusion of the Marxian model to broad segments of society.

The position of the "new middle class" in contemporary society is analogous in some ways to the situation of the artisan class in Salem before the Industrial Revolution. First, in both

[25] David Riesman and Howard Roseborough, "Careers and Consumer Behavior," in *Consumer Behavior,* Lincoln H. Clark, ed. (New York: New York University Press, 1955), pp. 1–18.

[26] Fromm, *Marx's Concept of Man;* see also C. Wright Mills, *White Collar* (New York: Oxford University Press, 1951).

[27] Daniel R. Miller and Guy E. Swanson, *The Changing American Parent* (New York: John Wiley and Sons, Inc., 1958).

groups, skills rather than productive property are inherited—
although perhaps interpersonal and intellectual skills rather than
craft skills are transmitted in the modern family—so that this kind
of "estate" need not be divided, and can instead act as a basis for
family solidarity. The fact that interpersonal and intellectual
skills are not necessarily sex-linked, however, diminishes the
male-female differentiation found in the Puritan-based family.
Second, the style of life of the "new middle class," like the Salem
artisan class, has set the standard for the society in facilitating
upward social mobility. In the post-Revolutionary New England
society, the artisans provided the ascetic model of Puritan family
life which has persisted in myth and legend. In contemporary
society, the mobile "organization family" prevalent in suburbia
points to the direction by which the family can facilitate upward
social mobility.[28] In this sense, the "new middle class" provides a
model for bringing up the next generation.

With World War II, the proliferation of large-scale bureaucracy—in both government and industry—heightened feelings of
powerlessness and a sense of exploitation. Under these conditions
the value of equalitarianism was strengthened. By the 1960's, the
increase in the bureaucratization of society and the lessening of
control over one's own destiny heightened ever further the values
of equalitarianism and collective security. Whereas the problem
of the Depression fostered an emphasis upon collective security in
economic areas, the powerlessness fostered by the bureaucratization of the '60's engendered strong reaction of youths and minorities to traditional institutions. This reaction is reflected in the
strong demonstrations against forced participation in the Vietnam
conflict, against systematic discrimination of minority groups in
education, industry and politics, and against the inadequacy of
university education for meeting the world's problems. These
actions symbolize a movement to abolish the traditional social
structure, defined by the emerging generation as irrational. Hence,
the "flower children," the disenchanted youth, the "hippies," and
the alienated in general have tended to reject traditional forms of
family life. These forms, they recognize, are intimately associated
with the political and economic system which gave rise to the
overpowering bureaucracies in the society.

Instead of discipline and hard work as virtues fostered in the
families, the dissidents have offered humanity, sharing, and love.
Instead of strictness in childrearing, they have emphasized "ro-

[28] William H. Whyte, *The Organization Man* (New York: Simon and Schuster, 1956).

manticism," with each individual expressing himself in his own way, "doing his own thing." They have drawn upon existing Marxian family norms devoid of sectarian, ideological underpinnings to experiment with new family forms.

PREMIUMS: MOTIVATIONS FOR CHANGE

Personal salvation, both secular and sacred, was the premium for conformity to ethical conduct under Puritanism. With a humanistic ideology, such as Marxism, the premiums are to be found in the development and expression of the distinctly human aspects of existence. This humanistic emphasis is apparent in the character of various social movements which represent the values apparent in the Marxian model of the family.

1. Status of Women

Movements for promoting women's rights occurred early in American history. The feminist movement was active as early as 1848, when, at a Women's Rights Convention, a "Declaration of Sentiments" was issued calling for the enfranchisement of women, full legal capacity of women after marriage, equitable divorce laws, elimination of the double standard in morality, equality of occupational and educational opportunity, and full participation in church government.[29] It may be noted however that this declaration did not embody a stand against the political and economic institutions as they were constituted in the mid-nineteenth century, but merely called for a reform pertaining to some special interests. In that respect the feminist movement was not intimately associated with the larger issues of humanism in an impersonal world. Rather, its situation was analogous to adventure capitalism (as contrasted with rational, bureaucratic capitalism) in that it would permit the remainder of society to continue much as it had in the past. (Rational capitalism, on the other hand, requires particular kinds of political and familial institutions to enable it to thrive.) In support of Marxism, Engels decried the subordination of women in the nineteenth-century bourgeois family. The accumulation of property as an aim in family life was

---

[29] Bernhard J. Stern, "Women, Position in Society," *Encyclopedia of the Social Sciences* (New York: Macmillan), Vol. 15, pp. 442–450.

imputed to develop "the welfare and advancement of one [males] by the woe and submission of the other [females]."

The twentieth century has shown a continued trend toward providing a legal basis and general consensus in the society for equal status between men and women. In general, state laws provide for equal property rights of husband and wife, equal rights for earning a living, and equal rights in civil law. As for social status, the feminist movement has set as its goal a "unisex" society, wherein sexual differences in all phases of life are minimized. Marx himself regarded "the relation of man to woman . . . [as] the *most natural* relation of human being to human being."[30]

There has been a general decline in differentiation in the roles of husband and wife. The blurring of sex as a factor in the allocation of marital and familial roles has minimized sex differences in household tasks and childrearing. Relations between men and women are more egalitarian in dating, marriage, and parenthood than they used to be. Increasingly large proportions of married women (and particularly mothers) are in the labor force.

These changes are reflected in trends pertaining to relative age at marriage of husband and wife and participation of married women in the labor force. With regard to age at first marriage, the evidence is that difference in age between husband and wife tends to be decreasing. This trend is shown in Table 5–2, which displays median ages of marriage for men and women by their age in 1966. The difference in median age at marriage between men and women in the 65–74 age range was 3.4 years, whereas the difference for the 25–29 age range was only 2.5 years.

Participation of married women in the labor force has steadily increased. Whereas in 1890 only 4.5 percent of married women were in the labor force, by 1969 the percentage had increased to 40.4.[31] Similarly, the presence of children is declining as a factor in determining the labor-force participation of married women. Whereas only 12.6 percent of married women with children under 18 years of age worked in 1950, by 1969, this percentage had risen to 27.8.[32] This increase in working women represents a slow trend

---

[30] Marx cited in Fromm, *Marx's Concept of Man,* p. 31.

[31] J. D. Durand, *The Labor Force in the United States, 1890–1960* (New York: Social Science Research Council, 1948), pp. 216–217. *Statistical Abstract of the United States, 1970,* Table 330, p. 223.

[32] *Statistical Abstract of the United States, 1970,* Table 331, p. 223.

TABLE 5–2 MEDIAN AGES AT FIRST MARRIAGE,
BY AGE IN 1966 AND SEX,
FOR THE UNITED STATES: MARCH, 1966*

	Male		Female	
Age in 1966	Median	Interquartile range (years)	Median	Interquartile range (years)
20 to 24	—	—	20.2	—
25 to 29	22.5	4.6	20.0	4.2
30 to 34	22.9	5.5	20.2	4.6
35 to 39	23.3	5.8	20.4	4.7
40 to 44	23.7	5.4	21.5	5.3
45 to 49	24.7	6.2	22.1	6.0
50 to 54	25.2	7.4	22.4	7.1
55 to 64	25.3	7.9	21.9	7.4
65 to 74	25.3	7.0	21.9	6.5

Note: Based on data by single years of age at first marriage. Percent ultimately marrying used to calculate these values is percent first married before age 45. *Source:* Based on answers to March 1966 Current Population Survey question on date of first marriage. The data cover the population of the United States, except for members of the armed forces living in barracks and similar quarters, who are not included in the survey.

From Robert Parke, Jr. and Paul Glick, "Prospective Changes in Marriage and the Family," *Journal of Marriage and the Family* 29 (1967), Table 1, p. 251.

toward de-emphasis of sex differentiation in work. This trend was strengthened by anti-discrimination court decisions with regard to hiring policies. Moreover, as automation of industry increases, the need for heavy labor will give way more and more to tasks which can be performed with at least equal ability by women. Hence, the trend toward the blurring of sex distinctions in American society can be expected to continue, possibly at an increasing rate.

2. Mental Health

One of the premiums which Marxian ideology envisions as a consequence of adherence to its precepts is the attainment of mental health. There had been concern over the treatment of the mentally ill throughout the nineteenth century. Dorothea Dix led the crusade for providing mental hospitals and therapeutic care for the mentally ill. By the twentieth century interest was manifest in preventive medicine and the maintenance of mental hygiene.

Until the Depression, however, the mental health movement was concerned with personal adjustment and individual therapy. But with the onset of the Depression, inquiry was made into the social context of mental illness. Particular attention was then given to the family. After World War II, mental illness was regarded as a major problem in public health, more serious than some physical illnesses in its consequences for the human resources in society.

The shift in interests to social conditions pertaining to mental health facilitated the integration of a Marxian perspective with other humanistic ideologies, such as Freudianism. The fruition of this integration appears to have developed only during the 1960's with the rebellion of youth against what they see as bureaucratic suppression in a modern society dominated by centers of control far removed from the mass of the population. If the new generation has psychological "hang-ups" and chronic anxieties, the basis lies in the willingness of parents (according to the interpretation by the youth) to accede to the demands of the bureaucratic structure and to organize their lives and the lives of their families, either through hypocrisy or self-delusion, in terms of these demands. Implicit in this rebellion is the strong premium placed on mental health and self-expression as criteria for evaluating family life. These criteria achieve greater importance than community status or economic achievement.

3. Experience as Enrichment

Most humanistic doctrines propose that each individual develop in a manner which will maximize the quantity and quality of those experiences which make his life "meaningful." In this context, meaningfulness can refer to a variety of ends— intellectual stimulation, devotion to a cause, obtaining pleasure, and other goals which are associated with self-fulfillment. From this perspective, Engels has suggested, that marriage is moral only as long as love lasts, and when fondness ceases, or a new passionate love comes along, separation is a blessing for both husband and wife and for society.[33] From a Freudian perspective, moreover, the kind of family life that demands constant suppression of impulses and goals is the nursery of neuroticism, and such a family group might be better off dispersing. According to this ethic, boredom, repression, suppression of desires, irrelevance of

---

[33] Engels, *Origin of the Family*, p. 73.

activities to ongoing social movements, and other ways of denying fulfillment are evil; they are the obverse of "meaningful" experience.

CONCLUSION

In the American context (as well as in some European countries), various experimental family forms have been developed in relation to status of women, mental health, and personal enrichment. The intellectual climate in which these forms have emerged involves the decline of the "natural-family" paradigm. This decline permits an exploration of new family forms for seeking enrichment of experience which are not constrained by a fixed set of theological or naturalistic ends of family life. Instead, the experimenters have allowed the kinds of experience they seek to determine the functions of families. Bases for experimentation include participating in the "drug culture," acting in a purposefully shocking manner, becoming "visible saints" in an effort to reform society, trying commune living (with or without group marriage), and desiring to live together as a married couple only as long as the relationship is mutually satisfying. Regardless of their source, experimental forms represent attempts to maximize the quality of personal experience, and they are often drawn directly or indirectly from Marxian conceptions of egalitarian family life.

It can be argued that the experiments in family living in the latter part of the twentieth century do not really represent inventions of different family forms. Many of these forms were applied in the 1920's and even earlier by utopians and by persons rebelling against American social conventions. However, these previous attempts occurred in a society still dominated by "natural-family" paradigms. The significance of the decline of "natural-family" presuppositions in law is that the emerging paradigms, symbolized by the Marxian model, permit a great diversity of norms, values, and functions of families in different segments of society. The newer family life styles fall within the range permitted under the legal-family model. Consequently, whereas the earlier experiments seem to have signified deviance by rebels, the more recent explorations in family forms may produce more lasting effects on American (and perhaps European) social structure.[34]

[34] Herbert Marcuse, *One-Dimensional Man* (Boston: Beacon Press, 1964). See also Herbert Marcuse, *An Essay on Liberation* (Boston: Beacon Press, 1969), pp. 88–89.

6

Family Variability: Cultural Models and History

To what extent is change in family norms constrained by "natural" functions? When all is said and done, it is this question which must eventually be answered. Let us now see whether the analysis of legal codes and the excursion into American family history has produced any solutions to this question.

First, this chapter will reexamine the presuppositions made at the beginning of the book regarding cultural models and analogies. It will then review and enlarge upon the findings of the analysis in terms of these models and analogies. Finally, we shall determine whether the findings have actually permitted some headway in answering questions about change in family and kinship organization in industrial societies (or at least in American society).

CULTURAL MODELS OF FAMILY AND KINSHIP

As the introduction to this book indicated, sets of norms and values regulating sexual intercourse and childrearing exist in every society. Ephemeral relationships (such as love affairs or babysitting arrangements) which might be created in connection with these activities are pauses in the continuity of society. For the most part, however, long-term arrangements have evolved. In the case of the family, these arrangements, emerging from biological relationships founded on procreation and birth, enable the society to persist from one generation to the next.

The relevance of biology to kinship is apparent in many ways.[1] Sometimes, the limitations on kinship organization imposed by the facts of biological relatedness are obvious: women do not give birth in litters of eight or nine; reproduction among humans is bisexual; women give birth to children of both sexes; the reproductive period of women is shorter than that of men; and the composition of groups related through birth and marriage is affected by survival rates. This set of arrangements gives rise to the fact that there are limits to the number of (using English terminology) mothers, fathers, sisters, brothers, uncles, aunts, grandparents, grandchildren, and husband and wives. A task in analyzing family and kinship is to discover how a society allocates activities, obligations, prerogatives, and privileges to these biologically derived statuses. The allocation of roles to these statuses might provide some insight into historical processes.

To regard biological relatedness as itself a resource suggests in turn an analogy: biological kinship may be viewed as the raw material out of which rules pertaining to social aspects of kinship are developed. As a resource, biological connectedness limits the kinds of changes that can be imposed by other aspects of the society. Biological relatedness requires a set of norms pertaining to marital restrictions, socialization practices of children, the manner of family guardianship in the society, and the relationship between familial and other institutions in the society. The configuration of these norms can then be identified as the cultural model of the family.

If biological kinship is regarded as a resource, a major question to be asked in historical research is: How does a society change in the course of utilizing this resource? At a given time, categories of kinship may be used in ways which sustain a highly differentiated system of social stratification; at other times, the organization of kinship relations may be oriented to integrating family units on an equalitarian basis.

One assumption made in this analysis is that, since organizing principles of a society tend to pervade its major institutions,

[1] David M. Schneider, "What Is Kinship All About?" in *Kinship Studies in the Morgan Centennial Year,* Pricilla Reining, ed. (Washington, D. C.: The Anthropological Society of Washington, 1972), pp. 32–36.

they can be regarded as strategies for integrating the society. Insofar as the principles which structure familial norms are isomorphic with economic norms, theoretical and methodological models which have been developed to analyze the economy can also be applied to family and kinship. Consequently, in the opening chapter of this book, several propositions treating persons as family property were set forth as guides for the subsequent analysis. The first two propositions pertained to the changing modes of marital exchange in highly industrialized, urbanized societies. Proposition 1 dealt with the shift from limited, segmented, and specialized markets to more extensive market conditions whereby the diversity of potential marriage partners is increased. Proposition 2 identified the change in the market mechanism that accompanied this shift as a change from emphasis on *supply* to a stress on *demand* in determining marital choice and anticipatory socialization for marriage and remarriage. We suggested that if the supply always exceeds the demand for qualified spouses, the bargaining position of the parental family as a supplier was untenable. The next two propositions then dealt with changes in family and kinship associated with the emergence of extensive marriage markets. Proposition 3 described a shift in the role of family and kindred from one of restrictive control over members' conduct to that of the sponsorship and facilitation of their achievement. Proposition 4 indicated that, as a consequence of this decline in restrictive control, the rights and duties of affines to each other are reduced. This reduction apparently results in a greater emphasis on the role of consanguineal relatives for defining kinship demands and duties. Together, the four propositions provided a framework for the analysis of family laws relevant to (a) the meaning of marriage and divorce, (b) the images of nuclear-family membership implied by alternative legal means of incorporating or excluding children, and (c) relative emphasis on marriage and descent in family continuity through inheritance of property. The legal analysis provides a context for interpreting more concrete changes taking place in the modern family.

FAMILY AND MODERN INDUSTRIAL SOCIETY

As modern social structure becomes more and more differentiated, the functions of families in the various parts of the society themselves tend to become diverse. This diversity results from functional differentiation, from particular historical events, and from demographic processes. First, as to functional differentiation, the increase in the complexity of economic and technological systems of the society creates great varieties of familial adaptations to the educational, financial, temporal, and locational conditions of work. Consequently, families might vary by (a) socioeconomic status, (b) work situs in business, manufacturing, education, public service, or profession, (c) migration or stability demanded by the kind of work, (d) occupational diversity *within* families, and (e) rate of upward or downward social mobility. Second, the multitude of historical conditions, conditions which have affected families differentially, also propagates large varieties of form of domestic life. Norms and values related to family life are proliferated by (a) ethnic origin, (b) region of birth, (c) rural-urban residence, (d) religion (e) educational background, and (f) major historical events such as wars and economic depressions. Third, family styles of life are variegated by demographic processes associated with urbanization and industrialization. In recent generations the following demographic trends have occurred: (a) lengthening of the life span, with a consequent increase in rates of widowhood, remarriage, and grandparentage; (b) generally lower ages at marriage, particularly for men; (c) increase in marriage and divorce rates; (d) increased participation of women in the labor force; and (e) overall lowering of birth rates.[2] Finally, effects of economic and technological change, historical conditions, and demographic processes combine to produce countless permutations of characteristics in the population.

The increasing diversity of family forms through (1) functional differentiation of modern society, (2) divergent historical and ethnic backgrounds of the population, and (3) changing demographic structure suggests also that family functions are becoming more varied in modern industrial society. Each combination of characteristics based on socioeconomic factors, historical background of families, and demographic composition implies a unique set of functions that a family is expected to fulfil. The marriage of an elderly couple, a young couple not planning to have children at all, or a couple with children from previous marriages indicates a different set of family functions from that implied by "natural"-family definitions which emphasize a strong

[2] Bernard Farber, *Family: Organization and Interaction* (San Francisco: Chandler Publishing Co., 1964).

marital bond and a clearly defined division of labor between the parents. Various studies have stressed (a) psychological therapeutic functions of the modern urban family, (b) economic sponsorship by parents and relatives, (c) companionship as an end in family life, (d) variations in the use of personal and material resources in meeting crisis situations, and (e) the complexities in the family life-cycles which require complicated strategies for meeting the needs of family members at different stages of their life careers.

The picture of the modern family contrasts sharply with the early American family. In colonial New England, "positive law, that is, the law made by man, was believed to have to comport with a higher, divine law for its validity. This idea of higher law, although later secularized, was to become an enduring legacy of the colonial period."[3] Some aspects of Mosaic law were thought of as natural and immutable; other aspects as modifiable and positive. The assumptions that underlay Puritan social theory in "the conception of the social convenant and the emphasis upon a God-given fundamental law were the genesis of ideals which flowered in the eighteenth century and shaped political and legal thinking in the early days of the Republic."[4]

In contrast to the Puritan conception that Election to Grace produces a natural hierarchy among men, the currently prevalent doctrines, that *all* men are created without differential status ascribed by birth and all are endowed with the same civil rights, assume a lack of "natural" institutional structure. A natural structure would imply that there be differential treatment between some men and others, and that those who support the natural structures should be rewarded, while those who do not should be punished. Presupposition of the lack of natural structure implies that any structure is created by man-made rules, which are then codified in law. Hence, in modern law one need not posit "natural" ends or purposes of institutions in providing for the perpetual continuity of social institutions. Particular "natural" ends become irrelevant inasmuch as institutions can continue to exist for reasons other than those that brought them into being.

Whereas the traditional conceptions of the family have presupposed a fixed set of functions derived from "nature," law in contemporary society is faced with the problem of providing

---

[3] George Lee Haskins, *Law and Authority in Early Massachusetts* (New York: Macmillan, 1960), p. 140.

[4] Ibid., p. 229.

continuity in social structures without presupposing fixed ends for these structures. To solve this problem, family law has had to assume that the perpetuation of social structures (such as the family) is desirable for whatever reasons people have. To accomplish this task, governments have had to modify laws which accommodate a variety of ends and which assume an equivalence of different value systems. These changes have included (a) a decline in the conception that "at marriage the spouses are assimilated, for many social purposes, into each others' natal groups,"[5] (b) the ending of provisions in adoption to provide membership of individuals in two families of orientation, (c) removing restrictions on support and inheritance rights of illegitimate children and providing them with ascending relatives, and (d) increasingly emphasizing lineal patterns in succession and inheritance (as well as in adoption). These changes follow the idea that all families have equal rights and standing in the society, and they thereby oppose the notion that congeries of families should be encouraged to continually fuse with one another in order to sustain homogeneous clusters on the basis of social class, ethnicity, or some other ascriptive criterion.

As the functions of family life become more varied in the different parts of the social structure, there is a necessary decline in "natural" law, which presupposes a fixed set of family functions. All ends of family life are then considered to be equally valid: within the constraints of the legal codes, people are free to experiment with family forms. In this context, paradigms of family and kinship consistent with a Marxian model have emerged in American society. This model, based on continual, free negotiation of rights and obligations in the family, provides for a maximum flexibility in experimenting with family forms. These experimental forms may at times overstep the limits imposed by law, and efforts are made through public opinion, police action, or some other means to eliminate them. Sometimes, as in the case of "swingers," where marriage partners are temporarily exchanged for the purpose of coitus, the deviants live a conventional family life in most other respects. In other cases, like communes, where persons may consider all commune members of the opposite sex as cospouses, the experiment in the family form is merely one aspect of a revolutionary style of life. In most instances, however, the increasing diversity in family functions

---

[5] Jack Goody, "A Comparative Approach to Incest and Adultery," in *Kinship and Family Organization*, Bernard Farber, ed. (New York: John Wiley and Sons, Inc., 1966), p. 58.

merely permits the introduction of nontraditional ideologies to reorient family organization.

CONCLUSIONS

For the most part, this book has used American family law as data in the study of family and kinship organization, and it has noted several consistent trends, which are described in the previous section. Now, we shall look at implications of these trends. The analysis of laws related to family and kinship as well as the historical discussion pertaining to the American family suggests the following conclusions:

1. The decline of the "natural" family

With the passage of time, the conception of the family as a social unit following "natural" laws which serve as an objective foundation for positive law is slowly dissolving. Based on earlier Biblical injunctions, the "natural"-family paradigm has emphasized nuclear family relationships which are normally associated with a fixed set of functions. In a sense, the list of functions presented by the anthropologist G. P. Murdock reflects the Biblical prescriptions pertaining to familial regulation of sex relations, reproduction (to replenish the earth), the proper socialization of children suited to the society, and the collaboration of family members in economic activities. These functions as an expression of natural law then act to regulate family life. Although some family forms, such as the Kibbutz family or the Nayar household, may depart temporarily from natural law, the logic of family functions predicts the ultimate resurgence of traditional family roles of parents and children. The view that the nuclear family is a natural, empirical entity assumes that:

> Marriage and the family are the foundations of our present society, as they were the foundations of all human societies. . . . Through all the changes and vicissitudes of history and development, the family and marriage still remain the same twin institution; they still emerge as a stable group . . . consisting of father and mother and their children, forming a joint household, cooperating economically, legally united by a contract and surrounded by religious sanctions which make

the family into a moral unit. . . . Any ambitious reforms aiming at either the destruction, or a complete re-creation of the family by means of external coercion and legislative changes on a vast scale . . . will, I am convinced, lead to the same result: a return to the old order of marriage and the family.[6]

Implied in the above discussion by Malinowski are the following presuppositions:

1. One function of the family is to supply the personnel to fill roles in the other institutions in the society—with the parents already filling these roles and the children preparing to do so.

2. The nuclear family is the most efficient kind of group which can perform this task.

3. The personnel needs of any society therefore sustain the structure of the nuclear family as an empirical entity.

In modern industrial society, however, the role of the family varies to a greater extent than ever before for the different parts of the social structure; this is so because of particular historical and ethnic influences, and because of demographic variations. Concurrently, families in different parts of the social structure have different kinds of specialization—with some families specializing in reproduction, others in the regulation of sex relations, others mainly in socialization, still others in companionship of adults, economic collaboration, and so on.

With a fixed set of functions as a basis, one could assume that the nuclear family is the basic kinship unit in society. Wider kinship structures would then be derivitive in serving to support the nuclear family functions. However, as families in the different parts of the social structure can be assumed to serve *different* functions, the nuclear family can no longer be assumed to have a natural basis. Accordingly, laws cannot favor one particular set of functions over others; instead, they must accord virtually all family forms an equal right to exist. Consequently, legal conceptions of illegitimacy, adoption, succession, and support tend less and less to presuppose the existence of a natural nuclear family.

Or, alternatively, suppose that modern technology develops to the point where large portions of the population are superfluous to the society's productive capacity, and it no longer needs all the personnel to carry on the business of its various institu-

---

[6] Bronislaw Malinowski, "Personal Problems," in *Marriage: Past and Present*, Robert Briffault and Bronislaw Malinowski (Boston: Porter Sargent, 1956), pp. 80–83.

tions—and with our increasing dependent or semidependent population segments, some observers believe that we are approaching this point. What then? If other social institutions no longer require the services of many people—if in fact they get in the way of the efficient operation of these institutions—it would be functional for the society if their family life no longer prepared them to fill organizational slots in these institutions, but instead socialized them to withdraw or to stay on the margins of society.[7] Under these circumstances, it would no longer be appropriate to insist that the nuclear family is any more efficient in generating members of the society than another family form. The nuclear family would then too decline as the ideal societal model in favor of a more flexible model.

2. Marriage and Descent

Why do social structures persist? Some social scientists, like Lévi-Strauss, suggest that formalized reciprocities form the basis for continued interaction.[8] Across the range of societies, marriage as an institution acts to create reciprocities between family groups and to inhibit conflict between them. In his analysis of those societies which prescribe cross-cousin marriage, Lévi-Strauss intended to show how social structures larger than the small consanguineous band draw their form from patterns of exchange of women in marriage. For Lévi-Strauss, then, marriage is the fundamental exchange relationship in the creation of social structure.

Lévi-Strauss operates with a social-contract view of society. Marital exchange involves creditor-debtor alliances between families in which women and other property—for example, cattle—are commodities and hostages simultaneously. Assuming a natural state of war, the social contract permits self-preservation and mutual security of groups by placing limits on the freedom of man to engage in conflict and exploitation.

Other social scientists, like Meyer Fortes, take the position that the stability of social structure emerges from the axiom of amity, by which Fortes means the norm, found in every society, that everyone is supposed to act to promote the welfare of his

[7] Bernard Farber, *Mental Retardation: Its Social Context and Social Consequences* (Boston: Houghton Mifflin, 1968).

[8] Claude Lévi-Strauss, *The Elementary Structures of Kinship* (Boston: Beacon Press, 1969), pp. 52–68.

relatives.[9] This altruistic norm toward kinsmen constrains people from exploitation and open hostility toward their relatives. The frequent violation of this norm merely testifies to the difficulty of its enforcement.

The epitome of the norm of amity toward kinsmen is the parent-child relationship. Through doing their best for their children—sacrificing their own inclinations when necessary—parents ensure the continuation of the moral qualities of family and society. The proper socialization of children is, for Fortes, the most important task in any society that is to persist. Starting from the parent-child relationship, the basic process in building social structure is that of filiation—becoming a child to a parent. The modes of filiation in a society—to whom and how one becomes a child—then define appropriate forms of marriage, patterns of inheritance, and ties with kinsmen. Matters of illegitimacy and adoption are particularly important in establishing (or denying) rights of filiation. Lines of descent consist of chains of persons related through filiation, and Fortes' position is that filiation thereby acts as a stabilizer of the social structure it generates.

Who is more accurate, Lévi-Strauss or Fortes? What is the "glue" which maintains the stability of family and kinship institutions in modern society—the contractual nature of marriage, resting on the reciprocities generated by self-interest, or the norm of amity, which draws its strength from the acts of filiation and descent?

The trends outlined in the preceding section on marriage, adoption, illegitimacy, and inheritance law show the continual fading of the "natural" family as a cultural model in American society. These changes express a more fundamental revision in the extent to which marital reciprocities are expected to override other considerations. When the nuclear family is regarded as the basic cohesive kinship unit, "the marriage bond . . . is the main structural keystone of the kinship system. This results from the structural isolation of the conjugal family and the fact that the married couple is not supported by comparably strong kinship ties to other adults." Indeed, under this system, an adult places "strong emphasis on the marriage relationship at the expense of his relationship to parents and siblings."[10] Trends in family law

[9]   Meyer Fortes, *Kinship and the Social Order* (Chicago: Aldine Publishing Co., 1969), pp. 219–249.

[10]   Talcott Parsons, "The Social Structure of the Family," in *The Family: Its Function and Destiny*, Ruth N. Anshen, ed. (New York: Harper and Brothers, 1959), p. 252.

in the United States, however, suggest that marital ties are decreasing in strength. Instead, as changes in adoption and illegitimacy laws indicate, descent seems to have become relatively more significant as a basis for family and kinship ties. There is a growing imbalance between the precarious marital tie of husband and wife and the stable bonds among consanguineal kin. The historical tendencies toward a greater emphasis on descent hence imply that the principle of amity is perhaps more fundamental than that of marital reciprocity in modern kinship organization.

3. The Family and the State

A change toward the legal-family paradigm implies shifting relationships between the institutions of family and state. Modifications occur not merely through the internal adjustments of family members to their economic or social circumstances but also as a result of the changing role of government in modern society. The emergence of the state as an autonomous source of authority and control over the population of a territory has raised questions throughout history of the limits of its power. The view that the family derives its reason for existence from "nature" has in the past given it some immunity from governmental arbitrariness in the United States. It seems important in the study of change in family organization to now ask whether the family will retain this immunity as the legal-family paradigm becomes increasingly predominant.

In American history, the *Massachusetts Body of Liberties* in 1641 decreed that "no man shall be deprived of his wife and children, no man's goods or estate shall be taken away from him, nor in any way indamaged under color of law or countenance of authority. . . . Every man of, or within this jurisdiction shall have free liberty, notwithstanding any civil power to remove both himself and his family at their pleasure out of the same."[11] In his essay "Second Treatise of Civil Government," John Locke wrote in a similar vein:

A child is born a subject of no country or government. He is under his father's tuition and authority till he comes to age of

---

[11] In *The People Shall Judge*, Social Sciences I Staff, eds. (Chicago: University of Chicago Press, 1949), Vol. 1, p. 17.

discretion, and then he is a freeman, at liberty what government he will put himself under, what body politic he will
unite himself to. . . . The power that a father hath naturally
over his children is the same wherever they be born, and the
ties of natural obligations are not bounded by the positive
limits of kingdoms and commonwealths.[12]

Although the American constitution does not mention the
family, several articles are relevant for placing limits on governmental power. Article 3 prohibits the quartering of soldiers in
houses in time of peace; Article 4 deals with "the right of the
people to be secure in their persons, houses, papers, and effects
against unreasonable searches and seizures"; and Article 5 de-
clares that persons shall not "be deprived of life, liberty, or
property without due process of law." These articles serve to
protect family and home from arbitrary police power of the state.

The broad application of common law in American statutes
also operates to protect the family from the state. The rule that one
cannot be forced to testify against one's spouse is intended to
protect the integrity of the marriage bond; if husband and wife are
of "one flesh," requiring such testimony would be tantamount to
self-incrimination. The common law, in one sense, can be interpreted as protecting the family from encroachment upon its
so-called "natural functions" by government.

Modern sociological writings emphasize the growing specialization or narrowing of functions in the American family. These
writings describe the general decline in child care, religious
activities, economic production, leisure, education, and health
care within the family domain. Functions which particular families perform, however, vary with their resources. Throughout
history, families with greater resources have been better able to
fulfill their responsibilities to their members, and much effort,
stemming from egalitarian ideals in modern society, has been
aimed at a redistribution of resources.

Perhaps the hardest problems of libertarian policy concern
the division of responsibilities between the family and the
government. Liberal ideals include equality of opportunity—
or steadily diminishing inequality. This and other purposes
doubtless require governmental assumption of responsibilities once largely or exclusively those of families, notably as

---

[12] Ibid., pp. 90–91.

regards the health and education of children, and, also, substantial restriction on family accumulation of wealth. In either case, limitation on the freedom of families is involved; and hard questions arise of how egalitarian measures may be pursued without undermining the structure [of the family] at its foundation.[13]

This is the dilemma: if family functions describe a natural state of affairs, which are considered "good" either because they are sacred or because they are the most efficient ways of accomplishing certain ends, then the law should protect the institution of the family from encroachment by government. However, unless restrictions are imposed by government, families will vary considerably in the extent to which they will fulfill their functions (according to the standards in that society). Hence, any society which both regards the family as a "natural" unit and adheres to egalitarian norms finds itself in the impossible position of simultaneously leaving the family alone as a "natural" domain and imposing regulations on family life to redistribute resources.

The solution in modern society to this dilemma is to deny the validity of the argument that the family domain should be autonomous because it is a "natural" unit. Instead, if the family is considered a sub-unit of the state, then the government can justify regulation of family life in the name of the public interest. In England, as well, "the state now endeavours to exert control in areas which were previously acknowledged to be within the sphere of influence of 'the family', the wider kin group, and the local community."[14]

The growing emphasis on the priority of government interest over family integrity is indicated by the growing number of circumstances in which governments "'buy up' rights guaranteed by the Constitution." In January, 1971, the U.S. Supreme Court held in *Wyman v. James* that "periodic, warrantless home visitations by welfare caseworkers" do not constitute an unreasonable search within the meaning of the fourth amendment, but even if they were considered such a search, the visitation would not be unconstitutional. Instead, a caseworker's visit would be a "reasonable" search and, therefore, justified because of the interests of the state. Justice Blackmun and the majority justified the

[13] Henry C. Simons, "A Political Credo," in *The People Shall Judge*, Vol. 2, p. 414.

[14] Christopher Turner, *Family and Kinship in Modern Britain* (London: Routledge and Kegan Paul, 1969), p. 93.

reasonableness on the following grounds in *Wyman:* (a) "the
protection of and aid to dependent children, whose needs are
considered paramount," cannot be relegated to a position secondary to what the mother claims are her rights; (b) the home visit is
the primary source of information regarding eligibility to continue
receiving aid, particularly since the agency provided notice of the
intended home visitation and emphasized the need for privacy;
(c) the purpose of the visit is "benevolent," that is, "to provide
assistance and rehabilitative services"; and (d) the public, as a
provider of funds has a right "to know how [its] charitable funds
are utilized and put to work." Thus, insofar as the family's
interests are considered in this decision, it is the *child's* welfare
rather than the integrity of the family that is "considered paramount," an ordering of priorities which is more consistent with
the legal-family paradigm than the "natural"-family model.

The dissenters in the *Wyman* decision, Justices Marshall and
Douglas, however, place less emphasis on the "benevolent"
purpose of the visitation and more on the investigative aims. They
hold that *Wyman* resembles criminal cases, in which search
without warrant is held to violate the fourth amendment. Justice
Marshall argues that a major purpose of the visitation is to guard
against welfare fraud and child abuse, both of which are felonies.
He contends that "the home visitation is precisely the kind of
search proscribed [in criminal cases], 'except that the welfare visit
is a more severe intrusion upon privacy and family dignity.'"[15] In
their stress upon the possible punitive action which might ensue
from the visitation, the dissenters see the visitation as a threat to
family integrity, a position which has the "natural" family model
as its basis.

Since involvement by government in family life, as in the
Wyman case, may have many purposes, potentially benevolent as
well as punitive, there is much room for interpretation about the
constitutionality of this involvement. It is likely, under these
circumstances, that those jurists and legislators guided by the
legal-family paradigm will tend to focus upon the benevolent
purposes (for either family or the public); those holding to the
natural-family model will emphasize punitive potentialities.

[15] In Significant Developments section, "Child Welfare—Warrantless Home Visitation by
Welfare Caseworker Does Not Constitute a Fourth-Amendment Search," *Boston University
Law Review* 51 (1971), pp. 154–157 and Thomas P. Atkins, "Constitutional Law—Search and
Seizure—Social Welfare—Warrantless Visits by a Welfare Caseworker to the Home of a
Dependent Child Beneficiary Are Not Searches, But Even If They Are, They Are Reason-
able.—*Wyman v. James,* 400 U.S. 309 (1971)," *University of Cincinnati Law Review* 40 (1971),
pp. 157–162.

The problem of government encroachment on the family, as a violation of its civil rights as a "natural" unit, however, extends beyond the overt purposes of "search and seizure." In the course of this intrusion, the government may "seize" information about the family, which is beyond that sought or knowingly divulged. Electronic surveillance (such as wiretapping) provides an example. The Omnibus Crime Control and Safe Streets Act of 1968 permits interception of wire or oral communications for "investigation of specified types of major crimes after obtaining a court order" or, without such order, " . . . to secure information . . . to protect the Nation against actual or potential attacks, or to otherwise protect the national security." In 1969, there were 30 federal wiretaps authorized by court order and executed, resulting in 1498 interceptions.[16] It is unlikely that all conversations intercepted dealt with the criminal matters for which the court order was issued; probably only a few of them did. Chances are that only a few of the conversations revealed anything different from that discussed in the privacy of any home. Moreover, many callers whose conversations were intercepted were not themselves covered by the court order. Has the government encroached on the privacy of the homes of all parties intercepted unconstitutionally?

Recent court decisions, which reflect the functioning of the legal-family paradigm, suggest that such electronic surveillance is considered to be proper. Sometimes, as in the case of *United States v. Escander,* the government "knew only that the suspect was engaged in illegal narcotics activity. . . . No specific transactions were known to the agents, nor did they know who the other party to the conversation would be."[17] Yet, these interceptions have been justified as reasonable—and not contrary to the fourth amendment. To reach this conclusion, it is necessary to assume that, as in the legal-family paradigm, families receive their charters of existence from the state and do not constitute entities whose freedom to function naturally transcends positive law in importance for the welfare of the society. Ironically, as the family in America has become liberated from the norms and functions associated with the natural-family paradigm, it has lost its status

---

[16] William G. Deas, "Constitutional Law—Search and Seizure—Wiretapping—Section 2518 of the Omnibus Crime Control and Safe Streets Act of 1968 Is Within the Constitutional Limits of the Fourth Amendment.—*United States v. Escander,* 319 F. Supp. 295 (S.D. Fla. 1970)," *University of Cincinnati Law Review* 40 (1971), p. 165.

[17] Ibid., p. 168.

as a protected domain and has become increasingly subject to governmental policies governing educational and welfare activities, enforcement of criminal law, and economic stability. The legal-family paradigm heralds profound changes in modern family life which will be generated by the state in the course of its handling the vast array of problems facing it.

Future legislation and judicial interpretation may regulate marital selection (for eugenic reasons), fertility (for population control), childrearing practices (for mental and physical health), tenure in marriage (for the welfare of the household), and domestic privacy (for the general welfare of the community). Add to these the modifications induced by technological and economic development, the capriciousness of history, and the drifts in population composition and dynamics, and you have the nuances of future domestic life. What will the child of the eventual legal-family paradigm be like?

Glossary

Affinity The relationship established between persons connected through marital ties. Stepparents, stepsiblings, in-laws, and aunts or uncles by marriage are examples of affines in American kinship.

Ascendants Ancestors in a direct line; one's parents, grandparents, great-grandparents, and so on.

Ascending generation A person's ancestors and their collateral relatives classified by generation. His parents and uncles and aunts would be in the first ascending generation; his grandparents and their siblings would be in the second ascending generation, and so on.

Ascriptive Pertaining to a social characteristic or status routinely assigned to a person by virtue of his birth or marriage.

Bilateral kinship Descent system which links person with relatives through both parents. Generally, mother's and father's relatives are given equal treatment and have equal rights and obligations with regard to EGO.

Canon law A body of Roman Catholic ecclesiastical law, generally laid down in decrees of the Pope and statutes of councils, which relate to those matters over which the Church claims proper jurisdiction.

Civil-law system   Codified bodies of law modelled after the system of jurisprudence of the Roman Empire, particularly as set forth in the Justinian code and its successors, a codification in recent times being the Code Napoleon.

Cognatic kin   Persons identified as related by genealogical ties, without particular emphasis given to mother's or father's line of descent.

Collateral relatives   Two persons with a common ancestor, but where one is not himself an ancestor of the other. For example, siblings, cousins, or aunt and nephew.

Common law   A slowly evolving body of statutes and juristic theory that developed with the court system in England, its basis being primarily court decisions that have served as legal precedents.

Community property   Legal system under which possessions are owned in common by husband and wife as a marital partnership, in contrast to systems permitting independent ownership by husband or wife or systems designating the husband as legal owner of all marital property. In southwestern U.S., derived from Spanish and Mexican law.

Consanguinity   The condition of being of the "same blood"; relationship existing between persons by their descent from a common ancestor.

Cross-cousin marriage   A marriage in which one spouse's father is the brother of the other spouse's mother.

Curtesy   In common law, the right of a widower in the lands of his dead wife.

Descendants   Persons for whom one is an ancestor: one's children, grandchildren, great-grandchildren, and so on.

Descending generation   EGO's descendants and their collateral relatives classified by generation. His children and nephews and nieces would be in the first descending generation; his grandchildren would be in the second descending generation, and so on.

Descent   A chain of parents and children through a series of generations. In inheritance, the passing of property to an heir.

Differentiation   The growth or development of roles or structures which supply complementary contributions to the functioning of a society or institution. Opposed to segmentation, whereby two or more distinct units perform the same function.

Disown   To renounce a relationship to a kinsman, who may be an heir.

Divorce   The dissolution of a marriage contract between husband and wife by process of law as distinct from legal separation without complete dissolution of the marriage or desertion of a spouse without legal process.

Dower   In common law, that portion of man's estate which his widow received for life, after which it reverted to his heirs. Generally statutes have eliminated life estates (q.v.) in favor of ownership which includes transmission of the property to heirs.

EGO   The person whose viewpoint is used to describe genealogical relationships in a kinship system. For example, "mother" is his mother, "maternal grandmother" is his mother's mother, and so on.

Endogamy   The marriage rule according to which a man is constrained to take a wife from within his own tribe, clan, community, or group. Although any marriage will be endogamous with respect to one criterion but not another, usually a society will consider only certain criteria important (e.g., race or caste).

Entail   To settle an estate on a series of heirs in succession so that it cannot be sold or bequeathed at pleasure by any one possessor.

Estate   The degree, nature, extent, and quality of interest or ownership that one has in lands, tenements, or any other effects.

Exogamy   The marriage rule according to which a man is constrained to take a wife outside his own tribe, clan, community, or group.

Family of orientation   The nuclear family unit viewed from the perspective of an individual reared in it and consisting of his (or her) mother, father, and siblings.

Family of procreation   The nuclear family unit viewed from the perspective of one of the parents and consisting of his (or her) spouse and children.

Filiation   The act or condition of becoming a legitimate son or daughter.

Genealogy   A mapping of ancestors, their descendants and collateral relatives, as well as persons related by marriage, indicating the siblings, parents, and spouse for each person.

Illegitimate   Refers to a child without filiation, neither born in lawful wedlock nor recognized by law as lawful offspring.

Incestuous marriage   Marriage between two persons who are related by a bond of kinship that is regarded as a bar to sexual intercourse.

Integration   Interrelations of persons or collectivities in which their sense of solidarity and their common interests transcend disparate goals and conflict.

Intestate   Without having made a valid will.

Intestate succession   Transfer of an estate according to statutory provisions which designate its distribution when one dies without leaving a valid will.

Levitical norms   Pertaining to norms of family and marriage found in the book of Leviticus.

Life estate   A property interest whose duration is limited to the lifetime of the person holding it and does not extend to his heirs.

Matrifocal family   A residential kinship group in which there is no adult male regularly present in the role of husband-father; instead, in addition to mother and children, there may be a maternal grandmother or other maternal kinsmen.

Matrilineal descent groups   Kinship groups in which membership is confirmed to persons related by descent through females from a common female ancestor.

Miscegenation   Intermarriage or interbreeding of different races.

Moiety   One of two equal parts; in inheritance, refers to estates divided so that one half goes to the maternal side and the other to the paternal side of the family.

Norm   A relatively specific pattern of conduct, the content of which defines obligatory or permissive relations between persons or groups.

Nuclear family   A married couple and their children (including adopted children), but usually excluding married children.

Paradigm   A pattern, example, or model that serves as an archetype in shaping one's thinking.

Parallel-cousin marriage A marriage in which the husband's and wife's fathers are brothers or in which their mothers are sisters.

Patrilineal descent groups Kinship groups in which membership is confined to persons related by descent through males from a common male ancestor.

Personal property Tangible or intangible possessions with direct economic value, except land and whatever is more or less permanently attached to or built upon it.

Polygamy A marriage involving more than one husband or more than one wife. The two kinds of polygamy are: (a) **Polygyny** One man married to more than one woman, and (b) **Polyandry** One woman married to more than one man.

Primogeniture The right of the eldest son to inherit the entire estate of his father.

Real property Land and whatever is more or less permanently attached to or built upon it.

Residence principle Formation of kin groups or communities on the basis of rules governing the location of married couples. With patrilocal residence, the couples live near the husband's father; with matrilocal residence, near the wife's mother; with bilocal or utrolocal residence, near either one, depending upon the relative advantages offered; and with neolocal residence, anywhere. Virilocal residence refers to proximity to the husband's kinsmen and uxorolocal residence to proximity to the wife's kinsmen. After several generations under the same rule, residential groups may be extensive.

Role A series of obligations to perform activities in connection with the social status of persons with whom one interacts.

Social status A position in a collectivity, (such as teacher in a school, mother in a family, or manager of a factory), which has attached to it certain rights regarding: (a) authority over others, (b) remuneration or reward, (c) a degree of prestige, and (d) privileges or immunities.

Statute A law enacted by the legislative branch of a government.

Stirps Stock, or line of descent. "Succession per stirpes" — One's succeeding to property by right of representing a parent who would have inherited if he (or she) were still alive.

Symbolic property   Those intangible things, such as one's genealogy, social contacts, or family reputation, which one accumulates by virtue of his birth into a family and which may affect his destiny but has no direct economic value. The totality of this intangible property may be regarded as his symbolic family estate.

Testator   One who makes and leaves a legally valid will or testament at death.

Trust   The confidence placed in a person who holds legal ownership of property to use for the benefit of another.

Value   A conception or standard by which things are compared and approved relative to one another. The things compared include feelings, ideas, actions, qualities, objects, persons, groups, goals, and means.

Will   An instrument by which a person indicated his wishes regarding the disposition of his property after his death.

Appendix

Year of Publication of Early Statutes Used In Historical Analysis of Intestacy, Illegitimacy, and Adoption Laws

State or Territory	Years of Publication or Passage	State or Territory	Years of Publication or Passage
Alabama	1823;1852	Nebraska	1855;1881;1885
Alaska	1900;1907	Nevada	1861;1912
Arizona	1865;1871;1901	New Hampshire	1745;1853;1891
Arkansas	1835;1837;1937	New Jersey	1800;1877
California	1850;1872;1876	New Mexico	1865;1871;1897
Colorado	1861;1883	New York	1786;1859;1875
Connecticut	1749;1786;1824;1866	North Carolina	1836–7;1873
Delaware	1797;1855;1915	North Dakota	1868;1877;1895
Florida	1829;1839;1892	Ohio	1833;1854
Georgia	1810;1851;1873	Oklahoma	1890;1893
Hawaii	1859	Oregon	1864;1887
Idaho	1864;1919	Pennsylvania	1810;1855;1872
Illinois	1829;1837;1858;1874	Rhode Island	1798;1857;1882
Indiana	1807;1870	South Carolina	1794;1870
Iowa	1839;1873;1901	South Dakota	1868;1877;1901
Kansas	1855;1859;1889	Tennessee	1836;1851;1858
Kentucky	1796;1860;1881	Texas	1848;1876
Louisiana	1808;1864;1867;1876	Utah	1852;1876;1907
Maine	1822;1847;1857;1871	Vermont	1851;1862;1863
Maryland	1787;1825;1860;1904	Virginia	1792;1856;1904
Massachusetts	1836;1882	Washington	1860;1881;1891;1911
Michigan	1818;1857;1872	West Virginia	1856;1913
Minnesota	1849;1866;1878	Wisconsin	1858
Mississippi	1848;1857	Wyoming	1869;1910
Missouri	1824;1855;1866;1878;	Dakota Territory	1868;1877
Montana	1866;1871;1895	Northwest Territory	1800

Selected Readings

[Books available in paperbound editions are indicated by an asterisk.]

Anthropological and sociological writings abound with general statements about the nature of family and kinship organization. Robin Fox, *Kinship and Marriage** (Baltimore: Penguin Books, 1967) presents an unusually lucid discussion. Other basic readings are A. R. Radcliffe-Brown, "Introduction," in *African Systems of Kinship and Marriage** (New York: Oxford University Press, 1950), A. R. Radcliffe-Brown and Daryll Forde, eds., pp. 1–85; George P. Murdock, *Social Structure** (New York: Macmillan, 1949); Morris Zelditch, Jr., "Cross-Cultural Analyses of Family Structure," in *Handbook of Marriage and the Family,* Harold T. Christensen, ed., (Chicago: Rand McNally and Co., 1964), pp. 462–500; David M. Schneider, "What Is Kinship All About?" in *Kinship Studies in the Morgan Centennial Year,** Priscilla Reining, ed. (Washington, D.C.: Anthropological Society of Washington, 1972), pp. 32–63 and A. R. Radcliffe-Brown, *Structure and Function in Primitive Society** (New York: Free Press, 1952).

Especially significant recent statements about family, kinship, and social structure are Claude Lévi-Strauss, *The Elementa-*

ry Structures of Kinship* (Boston: Beacon Press, 1969) and Meyer
Fortes, *Kinship and the Social Order* (Chicago: Aldine Publishing
Co., 1969). Commentaries on the positions taken by Lévi-Strauss
and Fortes appear in Rodney Needham, *Structure and Sentiment**
(Chicago: University of Chicago Press, 1962); George C. Homans
and David M. Schneider, *Marriage, Authority, and Final Causes*
(New York: Free Press, 1955); and E. R. Leach, *Rethinking
Anthropology** (New York: Humanities Press, Inc., 1966).

Many articles are devoted to the controversy over whether or
not the nuclear family is a universal natural entity. Some of these
are Marion J. Levy, Jr. and Lloyd A. Fallers, "The Family: Some
Comparative Considerations," *American Anthropologist* 67 (Aug-
ust, 1959), pp. 647–651; Ira L. Reiss, "The Universality of the
Family: A Conceptual Analysis," *Journal of Marriage and the
Family* 27 (November, 1965), pp 443–453; Richard N. Adams,
"An Inquiry into the Nature of the Family," in *Essays in the
Science of Culture,** Gertrude E. Dole and Robert L. Carneiro, eds.
(New York: Crowell, 1960), pp. 35–49; and Norman W. Bell and
Ezra F. Vogel, eds., *A Modern Introduction to the Family* (New
York: Free Press, 1968), Part 1, pp. 37–110.

Related to the basis for the nuclear family and kinship
organization are questions concerning the incest taboo and re-
strictions on incestuous marriage. Contributors to the analysis of
incest and incestuous marriage include David Aberle et al., "The
Incest Taboo and the Mating Patterns of Animals," *American
Anthropologist* 65 (1963), pp. 253–265; Talcott Parsons, "The
Incest Taboo in Relation to Social Structure and the Socialization
of the Child," *British Journal of Sociology* 5 (1954), pp. 101–117;
Mariam K. Slater, "Ecological Factors in the Origin of Incest,"
American Anthropologist 61 (1959), pp. 1042–1059; Robin Fox,
"Sibling Incest," *British Journal of Sociology* 13 (1962), pp.
128–150; Jack Goody, "A Comparative Approach to Incest and
Adultery," *British Journal of Sociology* 7 (1956), pp. 286–305;
Russell Middleton, "Brother-Sister and Father-Daughter Marriage
in Ancient Egypt," *American Sociological Review* 27 (1962), pp.
603–611; and Leslie A. White, "The Definition and Prohibition of
Incest," *American Anthropologist* 50 (1958), pp. 416–435.

Analyses of family and kinship organization in modern
industrial societies appear in Jesse R. Pitts, "The Structural
Functional Approach," in *Handbook of Marriage and the Family,*
Christensen, ed., pp. 51–124; David M. Schneider, *American
Kinship** (Englewood, N.J.: Prentice-Hall, 1968); Ethel Shanas and
Gordon F. Streib, eds., *Social Structure and the Family: Genera-*

tional Relations (Englewood, N.J.: Prentice-Hall, 1965); C. C. Harris, ed., *Readings in Kinship in Urban Society** (New York: Pergamon Press, 1970); Talcott Parsons, "The Kinship System in the Contemporary United States," *American Anthropologist* 45 (1943), pp. 22–38; Christopher Turner, *Family and Kinship in Modern Britain** (London: Routledge and Kegan Paul, 1969); William J. Goode, *World Revolution and Family Patterns** (New York: Macmillan, 1963); and Bernard Farber, *Family: Organization and Interaction* (San Francisco: Chandler Publishing Co., 1964).

Concrete studies of kinship in modern society often throw considerable light upon more general relationships between family and society. These include Elizabeth Bott, *Family and Social Network** (New York: Free Press, 1971, Second Edition); R. Firth, J. Hubert, and A. Forge, *Families and their Relatives, Kinship in a Middle-Class Sector of London: An Anthropological Study* (London: Routledge and Kegan Paul, 1969); Bert N. Adams, *Kinship in an Urban Setting** (Chicago: Markham Publishing Co., 1968); Michael Young and Peter Willmott, *Family and Kinship in East London** (Baltimore: Penguin Books, 1957); Hope J. Leichter and William E. Mitchell, *Kinship and Casework* (New York: Russell Sage Foundation, 1967); John Mogey, *Family and Neighborhood* (New York: Oxford University Press, 1956); Bernard Farber, *Kinship and Class: A Midwestern Study* (New York: Basic Books, 1971); E. Digby Baltzell, *Philadelphia Gentlemen** (Chicago: Quandrangle Books edition, 1971); Ethel Shanas et al., *Old People in Three Industrial Societies* (New York; Atherton, 1968); Robert F. Winch, "Some Observations on Extended Familism in the United States," in *Selected Studies in Marriage and the Family,** Robert F. Winch and Louis W. Goodman, eds. (New York: Holt, Rinehart and Winston, 1968), pp. 127–138; Reuben Hill et al., *Family Development in Three Generations* (Cambridge, Mass.: Schenkman, 1970); Remi Clignet, *Many Wives, Many Powers: Authority and Power in Polygynous Families* (Evanston: Northwestern University Press, 1970); and Robert W. Habenstein and Allan D. Coult, *The Function of Extended Kinship in Urban Society* (Kansas City, Mo.: Community Studies, Inc., 1965).

Other facets of modern family life are reported in such research monographs as Hyman Rodman, *Lower-Class Families: The Culture of Poverty in Negro Trinidad** (New York: Oxford University Press, 1971); Louis Kriesberg, *Mothers in Poverty: A Study of Fatherless Families* (Chicago: Aldine, 1970); Elliot Liebow, *Tally's Corner** (Boston: Little Brown and Co., 1967);

Mirra Komarovsky, *Blue Collar Marriage** (New York: Random House, 1962); Melvin Kohn, *Class and Conformity* (Homewood, Ill.: Dorsey Press, 1969); Daniel Miller and Guy E. Swanson, *The Changing American Parent* (New York: John Wiley and Sons, 1958); Robert O. Blood and Donald Wolfe, *Husbands and Wives** (New York: Free Press, 1950); Helena Z. Lopata, *Occupation Housewife** (New York: Oxford University Press, 1971); Helena Z. Lopata, *Widowhood in an American City* (Morristown, N.J.: General Learning Corp., 1972); and Norman Bradburn, *The Psychological Structure of Well-Being* (Chicago: Aldine Publishing Co., 1969).

Most of the above monographs append a methodological note describing the research outline problems encountered in data gathering and analysis. These appendices enable the reader to evaluate the quality of the data and to gauge his confidence in the findings. iscussions of problems and methods of investigation of families also appear in Myron Glazer, *The Research Adventure: Promise and Problems of Field Work** (New York: Random House, 1972); Hortense Powdermaker, *Stranger and Friend** (New York: W. W. Norton and Co., 1966); Bernard Farber, "Studying Family and Kinship," in *Pathways to Data,* Robert Habenstein, ed. (Chicago: Aldine Publishing Co., 1970), pp. 50–80; Harold T. Christensen, ed., *Handbook of Marriage and the Family,* "Part 2, Methodological Developments"; and Raoul Naroll, "What Have We Learned from Cross-Cultural Surveys?" *American Anthropologist* 72 (December, 1970), pp. 1227–1288.

The most comprehensive history of the American family remains Arthur C. Calhoun, *A Social History of the American Family,* first published in 1919 and reprinted by Barnes and Noble, Inc., New York, in 1960. Aside from this monumental work, there are localized histories dealing with some aspects of the family model derived from the New England colonies. Notable among these accounts are Edmund Morgan, *The Puritan Family** (New York: Harper Torchbooks, 1966); John Demos, *A Little Commonwealth, Family Life In Plymouth Colony** (New York: Oxford University Press, 1970); Bernard Bailyn, *New England Merchants in the Seventeenth Century** (Cambridge, Mass.: Harvard University Press, 1955); Bernard Bailyn, *Education in the Forming of American Society* (Chapel Hill, N.C.: University of North Carolina Press, 1960); Philip Greven, "Family Structure in Seventeenth-Century Andover, Massachusetts," *William and Mary Quarterly* 23 (1966), pp. 234–256; Sumner Chilton Powell, *Puritan Village** (Garden City, N.Y.: Doubleday and Co., 1965);

and Bernard Farber, *Guardians of Virtue: Salem Families in 1800* (New York: Basic Books, 1972). With the release of the nineteenth-century decennial U.S. census schedules to scholars, however, historians of the family are now preparing materials on family organization during the period of intensive urbanization and industrialization of the United States. Early reports using these census data include Stephan Thernstrom, *Poverty and Progress, Social Mobility in a Nineteenth-Century City** (Cambridge, Mass.: Harvard University Press, 1964) and Stephan Thernstrom and Richard Sennett, eds., *Nineteenth-Century Cities, Essays in the New Urban History** (New Haven: Yale University Press, 1969). Numerous leads on careers of prominant families are provided by Edward N. Saveth, "The American Patrician Class: A Field for Research," *American Quarterly* 15 (1963), pp. 235–252.

Implications of the distinction between "natural" and "legal" aspects of the family in American culture are explored in Schneider, *American Kinship* (cited earlier). Schneider points out how the interchangeable use of the term "family" as a natural and as a legal entity affects the use of kinship terms and creates confusion about the boundaries of the family in everyday life and scholarship. In contrast to Schneider's work, a theme in this book is that the natural-legal family dichotomy is losing its force in American culture.

Much of the background for cultural conceptions of the family is to be found in religious legal codes. A description and commentary of Roman Catholic canon law appears in T. Lincoln Bouscaren, Adam C. Ellis, and Francis Korth, *Canon Law, A Text and Commentary* (Milwaukee: Bruce Publishing Co., 1966). Ze'ev Falk, *Hebrew Law in Biblical Times* (Jerusalem: Wahrmann Books, 1964) presents a discussion of laws regulating the ancient Hebrew family, while Erwin Elchanan Schleftelowitz, *The Jewish Law of Family and Inheritance and Its Application in Palestine* (Tel Aviv: Martin Feuchtwanger, ca. 1948) offers a more contemporary view. George Lee Haskins, *Law and Authority in Early Massachusetts* (New York: Macmillan, 1960) provides an account of the secular and religious sources of family law in Massachusetts colony.

The legal references in this bibliography are intended to convey some of the important aspects of various fields of family law without requiring specialized knowledge.

The most extensive compilation of family laws through the 1930's is found in Chester G. Vernier, *American Family Laws* (Stanford, Calif.: Stanford University Press, 1931–1938), presented in five volumes and a supplement. The first volume deals with marriage law, the second with divorce and separation, the third with matrimonial property, the fourth with parent and child relationships, including illegitimacy and adoption, and the fifth with such diverse matters as infants, aliens, drunkards, and insane persons. A supplement was issued in 1938 to bring the earlier volumes up to date. Unfortunately, there is no comparable recent compilation, although John Mogey, "The Formation of Images and Counter-Images of the Family: A Content Analysis of Legal and Sociological Literature," in *Images and Counter-Images of Young Families,** Clio Presvelou and Pierre de Bie, eds. (Louvain, Belgium: International Scientific Commission on the Family, 1970), pp. 55–70, does develop a typology of parental roles based on a review of American family laws.

Also extensive is the work Joseph Goldstein and Jay Katz, eds., *The Family and the Law* (New York: Free Press, 1965). In a volume that is difficult to classify, they have collected a large variety of articles consisting of court testimony, briefs, legal decisions, statutes, case reports, and writings of social scientists, philosophers, jurists, and social critics—all of which provide a broad survey of modern American family law.

An excellent discourse on modern divorce law in the United States and Western Europe appears in Max Rheinstein, *Marriage Stability, Divorce and the Law* (Chicago: University of Chicago Press, 1972). Rheinstein does show that strictness of divorce law is related to divorce rate. Nelson M. Blake, *The Road to Reno* (New York: Macmillan, 1962) describes the historical background of American divorce laws. The challenge to the strict divorce laws of the nineteenth century, when the natural family paradigm was giving way to the "New Morality," is discussed in William L. O'Neill, *Divorce in the Progressive Era* (New Haven: Yale University Press, 1967). Many legal and social problems related to divorce are discussed in Paul Bohannan, ed., *Divorce and After** (Garden City, N.Y.: Doubleday, 1970). An earlier, but still valuable, insightful analysis was made by Willard Waller, *The Old Love and the New* (Carbondale, Ill.: Southern Illinois University Press, 1967), and research findings on reactions to divorce appear in William J. Goode, *After Divorce** (New York: Free Press, 1956) and Jessie Bernard, *Remarriage* (New York: Dryden Press, 1956). An analysis of divorce law in which the author discusses the potential effects of marital breakdown as a ground appears in Jan Gorecki, *Divorce in Poland* (The Hague: Mouton, 1970).

Historical background and nuances of matrimonial property

rights in civil and common law are found in William Q. de Funiak and Michael J. Vaughn, *Principles of Community Property*, Second Edition (Tucson: University of Arizona Press, 1971) and W. Friedmann, *Matrimonial Property Law* (Toronto: Carswell Co., Limited, 1955).

The conditions under which people would have parental authority over children restricted by law are depicted in Julius Cohen, Reginald A. H. Robson, and Alan Bates, *Parental Authority: The Community and the Law* (New Brunswick, N.J.: Rutgers University Press, 1958). They found that people believe that the law should restrict parental control more when children reach adolescence. Protestants are more willing than Catholics to grant children autonomy, and urbanites are more willing than ruralites to do so.

A recent analysis of trends in illegitimacy law appears in Harry D. Krause, *Illegitimacy: Law and Social Policy* (New York: Bobbs-Merrill, Inc., 1971). Krause discusses illegitimacy in the light of constitutional rights to equality, a public opinion survey of attitudes regarding illegitimates, and European approaches to illegitimacy. The survey indicates that although most people favor equal rights for the illegitimate, persons of lower socioeconomic status are more inclined to be punitive in order to discourage illegitimacy.

Roy D. Weinberg has revised Morton L. Leavy's compilation of American adoption laws in *Law of Adoption* (Dobbs Ferry, N.Y.: Oceana Publications, Inc., 1968). Jack Goody, "Adoption in Cross-Cultural Perspective," *Comparative Studies in Society and History* 11 (1969), pp. 55–78, compares the functions of adoption in African societies with those in ancient Rome, Greece, India, and China. Esther Goody, "Kinship Fostering in Gonja," in *Socialization, The Approach from Social Anthropology,* Philip Mayer, ed. (London: Tavistock Publications, 1970), pp. 51–74, describes the institution of foster parentage and its possible effects on socialization in a society in which roughly half of the children are raised by foster parents.

An empirical investigation of issues involved in inheritance, testamentary freedom, the probate court, the probate process, and family continuity is reported in Marvin B. Sussman, Judith Cates, and David T. Smith, *The Family and Inheritance* (New York: Russell Sage Foundation, 1970). Although the findings refer only to Ohio, their implications are much broader.

Legal and moral aspects of abortion are discussed in Daniel Callahan, *Abortion: Law, Choice and Morality* (New York: Macmillan Co., 1970) and in John T. Noonan, Jr., *The Morality of Abortion, Legal and Historical Perspectives* (Cambridge, Mass.: Harvard University Press, 1970).

There has been some speculation regarding the future of the American family. Various conjectures of the future are found in Bert N. Adams and Thomas Weirath, eds., *Readings on the Sociology of the Family** (Chicago: Markham Publishing Co., 1972), "Part 7, The Family's Future"; John N. Edwards, ed., *The Family and Change** (New York: Alfred A. Knopf, 1969), "Part 3, Forecasts and Predictions"; Arlene S. Skolnick and Jerome H. Skolnick, "Rethinking the Family" in Skolnick, eds., *Family in Transition** (Boston: Little, Brown, 1971), pp. 1–32; see also in Skolnick and Skolnick, Chapter 10, "'Deviant' Life Styles" and Chapter 11, "Experimental/Utopian Forms of the Family." As editor of *The Nuclear Family in Crisis: The Search for an Alternative** (New York: Harper and Row, 1972), Michael Gordon has collected papers on communal families.

Entries in the Glossary in this book are based on definitions from a variety of sources, including textbooks on family law and an unabridged *Webster's New International Dictionary.* Other major sources are Ernest L. Shusky, *Manual for Kinship Analysis** (New York: Holt, Rinehart and Winston, 1965); Sussman et al., *The Family and Inheritance,* "Glossary," pp. 349–353; and Fox, *Kinship and Marriage.*

Index

1 2 3 4 5 6 7 8 9 10 11 12 13 14 15 16 17 1b 19 20 21 22 23 24 25   80 79 78 77 76 75 74 73